Wellness Activities for Youth

Sandy Queen

Help Youth:
- Learn to cope with stress
- Define personal values
- Improve self-concepts
- Develop wellness skills

Volume

2

WHOLE PERSON ASSOCIATES
210 W Michigan
Duluth MN 55802-1908
800-247-6789

Copyright © 1994 by Sandy Queen

Library of Congress Cataloging in Publication data 92-64003
ISBN 0-938586-98-X

REPRODUCTION POLICY

Unless otherwise noted, your purchase of this volume entitles you to reproduce a modest quantity of the worksheets that appear in this book for your education/ training activities. For this limited worksheet reproduction no special additional permission is needed. However the following statement, in total, must appear on all copies that you reproduce.

Specific prior written permission is required from the publisher for any reproduction of a complete or adapted exercise with trainer instructions, or large-scale reproduction of worksheets, or for inclusion of material in another publication. Licensing or royalty arrangement requests for this usage must be submitted in writing and approved prior to any such use.

For further information please write for our Permissions Guidelines and Standard Permissions Form. Permission requests must be submitted at least 30 days in advance of your scheduled printing or reproduction.

Printed in the United States of America

10 9 8 7 6 5 4 3 2 1

WHOLE PERSON ASSOCIATES
210 W Michigan
Duluth MN 55802-1908
800-247-6789

Sandy Queen, Sandy is the founder and director of Lifeworks Inc, a training/counseling firm in Columbia, Maryland, that specializes in helping people take a better look at their lives through humor, laughter, and play. She has developed many innovative programs in the areas of stress-reduction, humor, children's wellness, and self-esteem.

Sandy is known as a dynamic lecturer, humorist, and educator with a special focus on the child within each of us.

Sandy speaks with inspiration and humor. Her philosophy—Lighten up! This is the only life you have!

Sandy Queen may be contacted at:

Lifeworks, Inc.
PO Box 2668
Columbia MD 21045
301-796-5310.

CONTENTS

ACKNOWLEDGMENTS

Creating a learning environment that is positive, caring, supportive, and growth-promoting, an environment in which students come to know themselves better, develop positive self-esteem, and learn about and care for others—this is the challenge of teaching wellness to kids. Some facilitators are able to create this kind of environment quite naturally, but most of us can benefit from suggestions. It is in this spirit that *Wellness Activities for Youth, Volume 2* is offered.

I am indebted to friends for some of the ideas and activities included in this book, and I am greatly indebted to the many children who have given me ideas that really work because they are student-created. All of the activities in this book have been used with real kids and have succeeded more often than they have failed. I say that because no single activity will work every time with every group. The more you get to know your students, the more you will know what activities are likely to work with them. So don't be afraid to experiment to find out what works for you and for your students.

Sandy Queen
1994

INTRODUCTION

Visit any school and you will probably find that within their mission statement is some reference to the development of the total child. Schools have always professed interest in educating the whole child, but with the current high-tech boom, falling achievement scores, and the increase in the number of students not working up to their full potential, much of the focus on the emotional and social growth of students has been set aside in favor of stepped-up academic programs. What educators need to remember is that students who like themselves—who feel competent, self-assured, and valued—perform better in the academic arena.

Wellness Activities for Youth, Volume 2 has been designed to help young people learn about themselves, examine important areas in building a wellness lifestyle, and perceive themselves in positive, self-affirming ways. Students can learn to take charge of their lives by acquiring the skills, knowledge, and strength to identify and stand up for their own values.

The activities in this book focus on growth in all major areas of wellness—physical, mental, emotional, values clarification, self-responsibility, self-esteem, relationship building, substance misuse and abuse, communication skills, and peer pressure. They can be used as a separate mini-course within your program, as part of regular lesson plans, or whenever you wish to emphasize a particular point. Although they are primarily for students from the middle elementary grades through high school, many can be adapted for use with college and adult groups as well.

Use *Wellness Activities for Youth, Volume 2* to stimulate your thinking about what you can do in your classroom or with your group to make wellness class time an enlightening and enlivening experience for you and your students.

NOTES FOR GROUP LEADERS

Wellness Activities for Youth, Volume 2 can be used by a variety of people who work with youth—counselors, camp directors, scout leaders, parents, teachers, and youth group leaders, to name just a few. Any normal, fun-loving, creative, daring, kid-loving, risk-taking facilitator can create wonderful, creative, awe-inspiring, attention-getting, fun-raising, retention-building activities! These can be built into almost any program. You don't need any special qualities, other than good judgment, a sense of humor, flexibility, and a democratic leadership style.

Before using the activities in this book, spend some time thinking creatively about your goals for your class. Then ask yourself, "How can I help my students learn what they want to learn?" When you ask this question you help create a student-centered classroom in which students become active participants in the learning process instead of passive recipients of teacher-directed material. Although having students assume a measure of responsibility for their own learning may not be feasible in all academic programs, it sets the tone for successful wellness programs.

Creating an environment in which all students can be involved in planning and implementing activities—an environment that enhances student growth through openness, cooperation, trust, and interdependence—causes classroom motivation to soar, keeps discipline problems to a minimum, and helps you and your students achieve your learning objectives.

Remember, when you raise students' *attention* level by creating an environment that is stimulating and comfortable—and fun—you also raise their *retention* level because classroom experiences that are enjoyable are remembered—along with the content!

Keep notes on what you liked about each activity and what you would change the next time. Only you know your group, and fine-tuning is important if you are to obtain the best results from your efforts.

Group discussion will stimulate students to identify, clarify, and express their feelings and concerns in an open and accepting environment. However, don't be discouraged if your first attempts at building such an environment are met with less enthusiasm than you had hoped. It takes time to build a comfort level that will encourage students to speak freely and openly.

Whenever you use any activity, first explain what is involved, especially when you are asking students to share information about themselves and their feelings. Make sure students know that there is a "pass" rule, that they will never be forced into sharing anything that is uncomfortable.

Accept students' contributions without judgment, maintain a "you can do it" attitude, listen, listen, listen, and be supportive. Always have a "no put-down" rule. When students break it, let them know immediately. Many times, put-downs are used to cover conflicting feelings. Remind students—gently—that often the person who puts another down is the one who has the real problem. That usually quiets the heckler!

Avoid using grades for these activities. If you must grade, grade on participation. If your students show up, are breathing and participating, give them A's. Grades really serve no purpose when using these exercises. Grades tend to say that one person's feelings and values are more, or less, valuable than another person's, and making value judgements about a student's attitude is exactly what we need to remove from our programming. Besides, these activities are not meant to be primarily cognitive anyway.

THE FORMAT

The format of *Wellness Activities for Youth, Volume 2* is designed for easy use. You'll find that each exercise is described completely, including: goals, group size, time frame, materials needed, step-by-step process instructions, and variations.

   ☞ *Special instructions for the trainer and scripts to be read to the group are typed in italics.*

   ✔ Questions to ask the group are preceded by a check.

   ➤ Directions for group activities are indicated by an arrow.

   ● Mini-lecture notes are preceded by a bullet.

THE CHALLENGE OF TEACHING WELLNESS

Those who direct wellness programs for adults are often trying to get participants to CHANGE—change their eating habits, change their sedentary lifestyles, change their life patterns. However, when working with kids the goal is not to change them but to help them become aware of the choices they will be facing throughout their lives, identify those values that are important to them, and learn to make good decisions based on good information.

Wellness programming for adults often contains dire warnings: if you don't stop smoking, stop eating so much fat, stop sitting around and not exercising, etc., your life may be shortened by a heart attack, stroke, or some other debilitating condition. Those warnings may strike fear into the hearts of adults, but not kids. Young people are here-and-now oriented: they don't care what will happen thirty years from now (when they are old!) as much as they care what will happen right now. They don't ask "Will it help me live longer and be healthier?" They want friends, acceptance, a chance to belong. Wellness programming for kids will be most effective if it addresses those needs.

The life-threatening consequences of some decisions—for instance, acquiring AIDS from risky sexual behavior—should be presented, but not by using scare tactics and dire statistics. Adolescents operate under a special delusional system in which the main precept is "it can't happen to me." Because they don't respond to scare tactics, use real-life examples to help youngsters realize that it CAN happen to them.

IN CONCLUSION

Wellness programming for youth is a seed-sowing adventure; the harvest won't come for many years. Your goal should be to help students become knowledgeable about themselves and their lives and to lay a foundation for lifelong wellness as early in their school years as possible. Don't expect a revolution! Overnight changes in children's behavior are not likely. It takes a long time to internalize new ideas, values, and attitudes. But, the process can be a growing experience for you and your students, and that is what is really most important. It is with great pleasure that I bring this book to you, and I hope that the time you spend with your students in these activities will be positive and growth-enhancing. I welcome comments, criticisms, and ideas about how these activities worked for your group.

Sandy Queen
1994

ENERGIZERS, OPENERS, & GAMES

1 WELLNESS GRAB BAG (p 2)

This enjoyable activity helps students integrate what they have learned about wellness into a creative skit. (One or more class periods)

2 THE CHEERING SECTION (p 3)

This delightful energizer is a way for students to find lots of different ways to "cheer!" (5 minutes)

3 CONCENTRATION ON WELLNESS (p 4)

This game is a fun way to help students reinforce their knowledge about the various areas of wellness. (20–30 minutes)

4 LIVING SCULPTURE (p 6)

This lively energizer helps students bring their definition of wellness into focus in a creative way. (30–40 minutes)

1 WELLNESS GRAB BAG

This enjoyable activity helps students integrate what they have learned about wellness into a creative skit.

GOALS

Emphasize the many areas of wellness.

Provide an opportunity for students to integrate what they have learned about the various areas of wellness.

To have some creative, wellness-oriented fun.

TIME FRAME

1 or more class periods

AGE GROUP:

Elementary through senior high

MATERIALS NEEDED

Grocery bags containing four or five items each; 1 bag per group of 4–5 students.

Examples of items: light bulb, keys, alcohol ad, book, prescription bottle, football, hat, ruler, candy, band-aid, mirror, doll, diary, fruit, stethoscope, cookies, picture of a family, salt shaker, scarf, soda bottle, cigarette, heart diagram, rubber chicken, picture of doctor, cookbook, running shoe, drug literature, smiley face, seat belt, etc. USE YOUR IMAGINATION!

> 👉 *Try to include one item from each major wellness area—mental, social, physical, emotional, and spiritual.*

PROCESS

1) Divide the class into groups of 4–5 students.

2) Give each group a bag containing 4–5 items.

3) Instruct each group to create a three minute skit using the items in the bag.

4) Give each group time for rehearsal.

5) Perform and have fun.

2 THE CHEERING SECTION

This delightful energizer is a way for students to find lots of different ways to "cheer!"

GOALS

Encourage creative laughter.

TIME FRAME

5 minutes

AGE GROUP

Elementary, or any fun-loving group

MATERIALS NEEDED

Empty CHEER detergent box.

PROCEDURE

1) Inform the students that they are to perform various cheers when you open the lid of the Cheer box, but they are to stop abruptly when you close the lid.

2) Invent a list of cheers that the students are to perform: mummy cheer, fish cheer, monster cheer, cricket cheer, frog cheer, bear cheer, angel cheer, rabbit cheer, bumblebee cheer, etc.

3) As you open the box, call out the cheer you want the kids to perform. As long as the box is open, they cheer. When you shut the box, they must immediately stop cheering.

4) Ask students how they felt as they created new ways to cheer. Discuss the importance of emotional health to a wellness lifestyle and encourage students to find creative ways in their own lives to cheer for wellness.

3 CONCENTRATION ON WELLNESS

This game is a fun way to help students reinforce their knowledge about the various areas of wellness.

GOALS

Reinforce knowledge of areas of wellness.

Encourage teamwork and cooperation.

TIME FRAME

20–30 minutes

AGE GROUP

Adaptable for any

MATERIALS NEEDED

22 index cards; double stick tape or mounting putty; matching cards for the game (prepared before class).

PROCESS

☞ *This game is played on the order of the classic television game show "Concentration."*

1) On the blackboard, randomly arrange the cards that you have prepared before class.

➤ Cards should be positioned with the content side facing the board

➤ Attach either with double stick tape or mounting putty so that cards can be taken off the board and replaced as needed.

2) Divide the class into 3–4 groups.

3) Explain that each group will work as a team in scoring points.

4) Have each group choose a spokesperson for the team.

5) Give a demonstration of how the game works:

➤ Team A will choose two cards, i.e., card #5 and card #20. Cards are taken off the board and shown to both teams.

➤ If the cards match, Team A scores 1 point.

➤ If they do not match, they are replaced on board and the next team takes its turn.

➤ When all eleven matches have been made, the team with the most points wins.

6) Have teams draw straws to determine order of play.

7) Proceed with game as described above, with each team taking its turn until all twelve matches have been made.

8) Some suggested matches for concentration cards are below. Don't hesitate to make some of your own! Matches can be difficult or easy depending on the age group you are working with.

CONCENTRATION CARDS

Strength, flexibility, & endurance. .... *Elements of fitness*

Meat, milk, grains, fruits/vegetables. .... *The four food groups*

Heart, aorta, arteries, veins. .... *The circulatory system*

Leading cause of death in the U.S. .... *Heart disease*

The drug in cigarettes. .... *Nicotine*

Main cause of lung cancer. .... *Cigarette smoking*

A balanced approach to life. .... *Wellness*

Feeling good about one's self. .... *Self esteem*

Any chemical that causes a change .... *Drugs* in the way the body feels or acts.

Anything that frightens, excites, ... *Stress* or angers a person.

One glass of wine, one beer, or .... *Alcohol* one shot of whiskey has the same amount of this in it.

4 LIVING SCULPTURE

This lively energizer helps students bring their definition of wellness into focus in a creative way.

GOALS

Illustrate the definition of wellness in a creative way.

Promote cooperation and creativity among group members.

TIME FRAME

30–40 minutes

AGE GROUP

Upper elementary through high school

MATERIALS NEEDED

One piece of paper for each student.

PROCESS

1) Begin by explaining that each of us has a personal concept of what wellness is.

2) Instruct students to write their definition of wellness on a sheet of paper.

3) Divide class into groups of 4–5 and have members share their definitions with each other.

4) Instruct groups to develop a definition of wellness using the input from the individual definitions.

5) After developing a group definition, instruct each group to make a living "sculpture" of their definition using all the ideas of the group. The sculpture is to be made with the bodies of group members. (Allow about ten minutes to do this.)

6) Have each group demonstrate and describe their sculpture.

7) During the demonstrations, write key words on the board from the skits that define the wellness concept being illustrated.

8) Use these words after all the demonstrations to develop a classroom definition of wellness.

9) Discuss the following issues:

   ✔ What was the major concept in the definitions that were illustrated with the sculptures?

   ✔ Was any one area of wellness over-represented?

   ✔ Was any area under-represented?

   ✔ Was there a major focus among the group?

   ✔ After studying the key words on the board, what generalizations can we make about the definition of wellness?

VARIATION

For groups that may have trouble with the physical nature of the activity, you may want to have them create collages using magazine pictures which best describe their group definition of wellness.

TRAINER'S NOTES

TRAINER'S NOTES

AREAS OF WELLNESS

5 SPIRITUAL: THE FLAME OF LIFE (p 10)

This activity challenges students to search for meaning during meditation. (5-10 minutes)

6 MENTAL: THOUGHTS TAKE SHAPE (p 12)

Sometimes it is difficult to put our thoughts into words. Sometimes it's easier to symbolize our thoughts through our behavior or emotions. This activity uses a hands-on approach to emphasize how thoughts and feelings are interrelated. (2 class periods)

7 FINANCIAL: FINANCIAL WELLNESS (P 15)

This activity helps students look at their ability to handle their personal resources as a part of developing self-responsibility. (45-50 minutes)

8 SUBSTANCE ABUSE: PROBLEM DRINKING (p 19)

This activity helps students recognize some of the problems associated with alcohol use and abuse and encourages them to find alternatives to alcohol misuse and abuse. (45-50 minutes)

9 EMOTIONAL: THIS IS HOW I FEEL (p 21)

This activity helps students identify how feelings are held in their bodies and how feelings affect our lives. (45-50 minutes)

5 THE FLAME OF LIFE

This activity challenges students to search for meaning during meditation.

GOALS

Create an atmosphere of self-awareness and meditation.

TIME FRAME

5–10 minutes

AGE GROUP

Junior and senior high

MATERIALS NEEDED

Large candle, candle holder, matches.

PROCESS

1) Turn off the lights.

2) Light candle and place it where all students can easily see it. You may want to have them gather in a circle around the candle.

   ☞ *You may play some quiet music during this time to further add to the meditative state.*

3) Use the following instructions for the experience:

   ➤ Look into the flame of the candle and think about your life, your self-esteem, your wellness, your sense of meaning and purpose in your life.

   ➤ As you watch the flame, consider its significance in your life.

4) When 5–10 minutes are up, have students share their personal reflections and meaning from the candle.

5) Use the following points for discussion:

   ● Observe how little light it takes to dispel the darkness.

   ● We have a choice in this world. We can choose to be just like the candle and light the darkness around us. Remember that the most darkness you will run into is the darkness in people's minds.

- This darkness can take the form of fear, self-pity, anger, sorrow, and self-doubt.

- Think of ways we can bring light into darkness.

- Just one person with a candle of light can lead the way through the darkness and enable others to follow.

- Your "candle" can carry the truth about yourself and others.

TRAINER'S NOTES

©1994 Whole Person Press 210 W Michigan Duluth MN 55802   (800) 247-6789

6 THOUGHTS TAKE SHAPE

Sometimes it is difficult to put our thoughts into words. Sometimes it's easier to symbolize our thoughts through our behavior or emotions. This activity uses a hands-on approach to emphasize how thoughts and feelings are interrelated.

GOALS

Examine how life energy is affected by the pressures experienced on a daily basis.

Understand that thoughts affect our behavior.

Identify power sources in our lives that keep us connected to our strength.

Create a visual representation of a dominant thought.

TIME FRAME

Two class periods

AGE GROUP

Middle elementary through senior high

MATERIALS NEEDED

Baker's clay; manual egg beater; electric mixer.

PROCESS

1) Begin the class with the following discussion:

- Life takes energy; sometimes it feels like our energy is all used up.

- Young people often feel this way because of the pressures of peers, family, school, society—all pushing and pulling at the same time. It sometimes feels like you're being pulled apart and put back together again, doesn't it?

- What you think of yourself and your life will have an important impact on how much effect all of these pressures will have on you. Your thoughts are powerful in creating your life.

- Thoughts become reality because our behavior follows our self-esteem and our self-esteem is created by the thoughts we have about ourselves.

2) Make Baker's Clay: Mix 4 cups flour, 1 cup salt, and 1 1/2 cups water. Knead for five minutes.

3) Use the manual egg beater and electric mixer to illustrate the following discussion:

  - It's easier to mix this with an electric mixer than with a hand mixer because the mixer is attached to a power cord.

  - If we don't have a "power cord" in our own lives, we are going to have a tough time trying to get through the problems that will confront us.

  - If we tried to use the hand mixer for this process, we would be exhausted by the end of it. Exhaustion leads to unsatisfactory results and lower self esteem.

  - This electric mixer represents the energy in life through which all things are made. What are the power sources in your life? How can you keep a constant source of power flowing into your life?

4) When clay is ready, distribute a small amount to each student.

5) Since thoughts create form, suggest to the students that they think of their hands as their thoughts.

6) Instruct students to form the dough into some item that represents something they are thinking about.

7) Use the following points for discussion as they work:

  - Sometimes the things we would like to give form to are not easy to make, so we use symbols.

    ✔ What could you make to symbolize happiness? Frustration? Sadness? Peace? Loneliness?

    ✔ What are some of the thoughts you would like to mold into form?

8) Objects can be dried at room temperature or at 350 degrees for 60 minutes.

    ☞ *If students choose to make ornaments that can be hung, a paper clip should be inserted in the top before drying or baking. Completed objects can be kept natural or decorated with felt tip pens, enamel, water colors, or tempera.*

©1994 Whole Person Press 210 W Michigan Duluth MN 55802   (800) 247-6789

9) During a second class session, after items have dried, have students break into groups of 4–5 and talk about how their thought took form, and the symbols they used for their thoughts.

10) Questions for discussion:

✔ Was it easy or difficult to shape your thoughts?

✔ Was it fun or disturbing to try to get a thought or emotion into some form?

✔ Did working with the clay help release any tension for you? Did it help you see anything more clearly as you tried to symbolize your thoughts into some form?

TRAINER'S NOTES

7 FINANCIAL WELLNESS

This activity helps students look at their ability to handle their personal resources as a part of developing self-responsibility.

GOALS

Define and evaluate financial wellness.

Examine "needs" vs. "wants."

Understand the need for resource management as an important part of a positive lifestyle.

TIME FRAME

45–50 minutes

AGE GROUP

Junior and senior high

MATERIALS NEEDED

Financial Wellness worksheets for each student.

PROCESS

1) Begin with a discussion using the following points:

- Most of us could probably think of many ways they would like to handle a million dollars.

- You can expect to make that much money by the time you retire.

- Some of us may not even feel prepared to handle the money they have right now.

- A recent study shows that teens spent an estimated $30.5 billion on themselves in 1987.

- If you are an average teen, you spend about $1000 a year on yourself.

- More and more teens are working to earn their own money and have responsibility for the money they earn.

©1994 Whole Person Press 210 W Michigan Duluth MN 55802   (800) 247-6789

- In the U.S., about seven out of ten seniors and four out of ten sophomores are employed. The average working teen makes about $70 per week.

  ✔ How do you decide what to spend your money on?

  ✔ How much time do you spend planning how to spend your money?

- Good money management is an important factor in successful living. The money habits you develop as a teen can pave the way to future financial fitness or future financial "disability."

- It's not unusual to have trouble handling money. There seem to be so many things that we "need" to make life fun. Advertisers are constantly telling us how life would be better with their particular goods or services.

- It's easy for "wants" and "needs" to get confused.

- So, how does this apply to wellness? You thought wellness was just eating right, handling stress, and getting enough exercise.

- Being able to handle finances—understanding the difference between wants and needs—is part of being a whole person and a sign that you have taken self-responsibility seriously.

2) Distribute the **Financial Wellness** worksheets and give the following instructions for completing it:

  ➤ Write a list of 25 things you have bought in the last year, i.e., clothes, stereo, tapes or CDs, bike, etc.

  ➤ In the first column, *I Really Needed That*, mark the things that were survival items—things that were real needs. Ask yourself: Did I really NEED this item? Would life have come to a screeching halt without it, or did I just WANT it? Could I have borrowed the same item, done without it, or used something else?

  ➤ In the second column, *I Just Wanted This*, mark the things that were wants rather than needs.

  ➤ Total the number of NEEDS and the number of WANTS at the bottom of the page and record the numbers.

3) Discuss the following as a class or have the students break into smaller groups of 4–5 students for discussion.

  ✔ Did you have more NEEDS than WANTS or the other way around?

✔ Were you really honest with yourself about your needs and wants? Did you NEED those basketball shoes because you were on the team or did you NEED them because all of your friends had a pair?

✔ How did the issues of self-esteem and peer pressure figure into your wants?

✔ If your current wants *vs.* needs status continues into your adulthood, how financially well will you be?

✔ What kinds of plans are you making now for financial wellness?

4) Encourage students to write a plan for financial wellness on the bottom part of the worksheet.

5) Encourage class discussion of their plans.

☞ *This activity is particularly effective when combined with a visit from a financial adviser who can give the students some basic pointers on financial planning.*

TRAINER'S NOTES

©1994 Whole Person Press 210 W Michigan Duluth MN 55802   (800) 247-6789

FINANCIAL WELLNESS WORKSHEET

List below 25 things you have purchased during the last year.

	I Really Needed This	I Just Wanted This
1.		
2.		
3.		
4.		
5.		
6.		
7.		
8.		
9.		
10.		
11.		
12.		
13.		
14.		
15.		
16.		
17.		
18.		
19.		
20.		
21.		
22.		
23.		
24.		
25.		

My Plan for Financial Wellness:

8 PROBLEM DRINKING

This activity helps students recognize some of the problems associated with alcohol use and abuse and encourages them to find alternatives to alcohol misuse and abuse.

GOALS

Help students identify some of the lifestyle factors that may encourage problem drinking.

Examine ways to prevent alcohol misuse and abuse.

Aid students in making personal decisions about alcohol use.

TIME FRAME

45–50 minutes

AGE GROUP

Upper Elementary through senior high

MATERIALS NEEDED

Role description sheets (a different one for each member of the class; it's OK to use duplicate sheets in different groups).

PROCESS

1) Prepare role description sheets using the situations on page 20 or create some of your own.

2) Divide students into groups of 4–5 and distribute different role sheets to each student in the group.

3) Have each student talk about his or her reasons for alcohol use according to the situation described on her role sheet. Instruct each student to also talk about the pros and cons of her or his drinking and the consequences that could be associated with alcohol use in this situation.

4) The group will then suggest alternatives for the student and give suggestions for ways of handling potential alcohol problems that may be associated with the situation given on the role sheet.

5) Reconvene the large group and discuss the following:

✔ What are some of the pros and cons about drinking your group came up with?

✔ What were some of the possible reasons that the situations on your role sheet could lead to alcohol abuse?

✔ Will all of these situations lead to alcohol misuse or abuse?

✔ What helpful suggestions were given by the group?

✔ How do people like this affect all of us?

✔ How do drinking problems get started?

✔ How do social relationships help develop alcohol-related problems?

✔ What community services are available to people with alcohol-related problems?

✔ What do you think is the main influence on teens in their decisions about alcohol?

✔ What guidelines have you used for your own decisions about alcohol use?

ROLE DESCRIPTIONS

1) Teenage girl—goes to lots of parties; friends are important to her; many of her friends drink including her boyfriend.

2) Married couple—entertain a lot; have lots of friends; are involved in many social situations throughout the year; the husband's "big boss" is a heavy drinker and likes for his junior executives to be "part of the team."

3) Taxi driver—frustrated with not having achieved more in life.

4) Company president—under a huge load of stress both at home and at work; has no place to get away from it all.

5) High school student—wants to be part of the group; frustrated because he or she cannot seem to find a group to accept him or her.

6) Teenager—comes from a home with alcoholic parents; is yelled at and hit a lot; is generally depressed.

7) Middle-aged woman—all her children are grown and gone; she has no job outside the home; her days are long and empty.

9 THIS IS HOW I FEEL

This activity helps students identify how feelings are held in their bodies and how feelings affect our lives.

GOALS

Emphasize that all feelings are okay.

Differentiate between Thinking and Feeling.

Recognize the powerful influence feelings have over our emotional well-being.

Recognize that people react to feelings in different ways.

Identify places in the body where feelings originate.

TIME FRAME

45–50 minutes

AGE GROUP

Elementary through senior high

MATERIALS NEEDED

Feelings worksheet for each student.

PROCESS

1) Begin by having students brainstorm a list of all the feeling words they can think of.

   ➤ Write this list on the board.

2) Use the following points for discussion:

   ● Feelings can have a profound effect on your body. They can take you to the highest mountain peak or drop you into the lowest gutter.

   ● Feelings are okay—all of them. It's not our feelings that get us into trouble—it is what we DO with them.

   ● If you refuse to acknowledge your feelings, they can eventually make you physically ill.

- We give feelings labels, like the list we have made here—happy, sad, frustrated, depressed.

- The labels describe EMOTIONS, but don't tell us how these emotions are experienced by the person. For example, if you say "I feel sick," you probably feel nausea in your stomach, whereas, if you say "I feel really tired," the feeling is probably experienced throughout your body as fatigue.

- We often try to intellectualize our feelings by saying how we THINK we feel, instead of paying attention to how feelings are making themselves known in our bodies. If you say, "I feel everyone should eat good foods," that is a THOUGHT, not a FEELING.

3) Distribute **Feelings** Worksheets to each student.

4) Provide the following instructions for completion of the worksheet:

➤ In the place provided write down six feelings you experience most often.

   ➤ Put an asterix (*) next to the ones that are easiest to express;

   ➤ Put a pound symbol (#) next to the ones that are most difficult to express;

   ➤ Put an exclamation point (!) next to the ones that cause you the most problems;

   ➤ Put the letter **A** (for **A**lways) next to the one you feel most often.

   ➤ Put letter **S** (for **S**ick) next to the ones that have caused you to be physically ill when they have gone on too long.

➤ Use the number beside each feeling to identify on the body outline where each feeling originates in your body, i.e., fear/stomach (stomachache), fatigue/head (headache).

5) Ask students to reflect on the following questions:

✔ How does paying attention to where an emotion is experienced help you understand the emotion better?

✔ How many feelings originate in the same parts of your body?

✔ Do good feelings and not-so-good feelings come from the same places?

✔ Does your body ever give you signals that a particular feeling is on its way? Do you listen? What happens if you don't listen? What happens if you do listen?

6) To help students see how alike and different they are in their feeling experiences, have them complete the open-ended sentences on their worksheet and share with the group. Discuss the similarities and differences in how feelings are experienced.

TRAINER'S NOTES

FEELINGS WORKSHEET

List six feelings you have most often:

1.

2.

3.

4.

5.

6.

Write the number beside each feeling on the body outline below to indicate where each feeling originates in your own body.

Finish the following sentences:

*The place in my body where I experience most
of my feelings is* _____ .

My body tells me I'm happy by _____ .

My body tells me I'm mad by _____ .

My body tells me I'm sad by _____ .

*A physical problem that has been caused
by a feeling is* _____ .

GENERAL WELLNESS

10 WELLNESS THROUGH A LIFETIME (p 26)

Students look at how the importance of the various areas of wellness changes throughout life. (45–50 minutes)

11 THE WELL BODY (p 29)

This activity helps students visualize the "whole person" concept of wellness. (45–50 minutes)

12 QUALITIES OF SUCCESS (p 31)

Some of the same qualities that it takes to be a person who achieves success in life are also the same qualities it takes to lead a positive, wellness-oriented life. This mini-activity helps students identify those qualities they see as necessary for achieving success as well as achieving a wellness lifestyle. (15–20 minutes)

13 WINDS OF CHANGE (p 33)

This historical perspective encourages students to examine how the concepts of health and wellness have changed throughout history. (Several class periods)

14 YESTERDAY, TODAY & TOMORROW (p 35)

This activity gives students the chance to look at the results of positive and negative lifestyle choices that begin in childhood and follow us into our adult lives.(45–50 minutes)

15 FLYING HIGH (p 38)

This fun activity for younger children helps celebrate all the great things they are already doing to have a wellness-oriented life. (20 minutes)

16 ROLLING ALONG (p 42)

This activity offers a visual model of wellness and helps students appreciate that the more intricate their identity—the more things they have to identify themselves by—the more positive a life they will lead. (45–50 minutes)

17 WELLNESS JOURNAL (p 46)

This journaling experience helps students identify the ways they care for themselves daily in each of the major wellness areas. (several weeks)

18 WELL, WELL, WELL (p 50)

Students create a project that looks at the qualities of a well person. (1 hour)

10 WELLNESS THOUGH A LIFETIME

Students look at how the importance of the various areas of wellness changes throughout life.

GOALS

Examine the value of the various areas of wellness in an individual's life.

Examine various areas of wellness for their importance in individuals of various ages.

Compare group opinion about the ranking of wellness areas in various age groups with actual interviews.

TIME FRAME

45–50 minutes for initial class; follow-up class for interview evaluation

AGE GROUP

Upper elementary through senior high

MATERIALS NEEDED

Wellness Ranking Worksheet for each student.

PROCESS

1) List five major areas of wellness on the board:

   Mental—ability to adjust to life;
   Social—relationships;
   Physical—fitness/nutrition;
   Emotional—feelings;
   Spiritual—peace/meaning of life.

2) On a worksheet, have students rank the areas of wellness from 1 to 5 with 1 being the highest ranking, 5 the lowest. They should rank order according to the importance they see for these five areas in their own lives.

3) Complete a tally of results on the board and answer the questions below.

   ✔ Which area was chosen most important for this age group? Why?

   ✔ Which area was chosen least important for this age group? Why?

©1994 Whole Person Press 210 W Michigan Duluth MN 55802   (800) 247-6789

4) Now have the students rank the areas of wellness for a 10-year-old child.

5) Tally results and discuss their reasons for various rankings.

6) Now have them re-rank the areas for a 25-year-old person. Tally and discuss reasons for rankings.

7) Re-rank for a 40-year-old and, finally, a 70-year-old. Tally results and discuss rankings.

8) Use the following questions for discussion:

✔ Was there any ranking that was consistently high or low? Why do you think that is?

✔ What major changes in ranking occured during this exercise?

✔ What changes in health and wellness focus can you see occurring over the life of an individual?

✔ How do you see your own personal wellness focus changing over your lifetime? Why do you think that will happen?

9) Following their self-evaluation, have students interview people 10-, 25-, 40-, and 70-years old, asking those people to rank in order the areas they consider important in their lives.

10) Have students bring their results back to class.

11) Tally rankings.

12) Use the following questions for discussion:

✔ How did the actual interview results compare with what we thought would be important to people of various ages?

✔ Were there any surprises here?

✔ Are there any generalizations we can make about how wellness focus changes over a lifetime?

©1994 Whole Person Press 210 W Michigan Duluth MN 55802   (800) 247-6789

WELLNESS OVER A LIFETIME

Five Areas of Wellness:
    Mental—ability to adjust to life; self esteem
    Social—relationships
    Physical—fitness/nutrition/health
    Emotional—feelings
    Spiritual—peace of mind/purpose in life/religion

RANK ORDER THE ABOVE FIVE AREAS OF WELLNESS ACCORDING TO THEIR IMPORTANCE IN **YOUR** LIFE. (1 IS MOST IMPORTANT; 5 IS LEAST IMPORTANT)

1.

2.

3.

4.

5.

RANK ORDER THE FIVE AREAS IN THE ORDER YOU THINK WOULD BE MOST IMPORTANT TO A **10-YEAR-OLD**.

1.

2.

3.

4.

5.

RANK ORDER THE FIVE AREAS IN THE ORDER YOU THINK WOULD BE MOST IMPORTANT TO A **25-YEAR-OLD**.

1.

2.

3.

4.

5.

RANK ORDER THE FIVE AREAS IN THE ORDER YOU THINK WOULD BE MOST IMPORTANT TO A **40-YEAR-OLD**.

1.

2.

3.

4.

5.

RANK ORDER THE FIVE AREAS IN THE ORDER YOU THINK WOULD BE MOST IMPORTANT TO A **70-YEAR-OLD**.

1.

2.

3.

4.

5.

©1994 Whole Person Press 210 W Michigan Duluth MN 55802   (800) 247-6789

11 THE WELL BODY

This activity helps students visualize the "whole person" concept of wellness.

GOALS

Explore the concept that wellness involves the whole person.

Promote creativity and group participation.

TIME FRAME

45–50 minutes

AGE GROUP

Adaptable to any

MATERIALS NEEDED

Butcher paper for body tracing; markers for each group.

PROCESS

1) Before class, trace the outline of a student's body onto butcher paper.

2) Decorate the body with facial features, clothing, etc. You don't have to make it fancy; the main function of the decorating is to clarify to students which part of the body they have been given after it has been cut apart!

3) Cut the body tracing into pieces; legs, arms, head, chest, abdomen.

4) Divide students into groups and distribute body parts.

5) Give the following instructions:

> ➤ Brainstorm wellness behaviors and lifestyle habits that are important for keeping your group's particular part of the body healthy, well, and strong.

> ➤ Write your ideas on the blank side of your body part.

> ➤ Be creative in your thinking. Write down every suggestion, even the crazy ones. Take into consideration all the areas of wellness: mental, social, physical, emotional, and spiritual.

6) After 10–15 minutes of brainstorming, regather groups to share the wellness ideas they generated for their body parts.

7) As parts and ideas are shared, reconstruct the body by taping it back together with clear tape and displaying it idea-side out.

TRAINER'S NOTES

12 QUALITIES OF SUCCESS

Some of the same qualities that it takes to be a person who achieves success in life are also the same qualities it takes to lead a positive, wellness-oriented life. This mini-activity helps students identify those qualities they see as necessary for achieving success as well as achieving a wellness lifestyle.

GOALS

Identify characteristics of a successful person.

Identify characteristics of those who achieve a wellness-oriented life.

TIME FRAME

15–20 minutes

AGE GROUP

Upper elementary through senior high

MATERIALS NEEDED

Blackboard; chalk.

PROCESS

1) Begin by asking students to brainstorm a list of qualities of a person in life who has achieved success. These may include, but are not limited to, the following:

   Motivation
   Risk-Taking
   Perseverance
   Self-awareness
   Happy
   Responsible
   Goal-Oriented

2) Use each of the items listed and ask the following questions:

   ✔ Is this characteristic important in creating a wellness lifestyle? Why or why not?

✔ Is this a characteristic that you see as important in your journey toward wellness?

✔ Do these characteristics only show up during adulthood, or are they things young people can work toward now?

✔ Are there any qualities of a successful person that are not qualities of a well person or vice versa?

TRAINER'S NOTES

13 WINDS OF CHANGE

This historical perspective encourages students to examine how the concepts of health and wellness have changed throughout history.

GOALS

Observe philosophy of health and wellness throughout history.

Trace the philosophy of a healthy mind, body, and spirit.

Make some predictions about the future of wellness.

TIME FRAME

Several class periods

AGE GROUP

Junior and senior high

MATERIALS NEEDED

Library resources.

PROCESS

1) Begin with an opening discussion:

- Wellness has only existed as a concept since the late 1970's, but the philosophy of a healthy mind, body, and spirit has its roots in early history.

- The concept of a sound mind in a sound body began with the early Greeks.

- Ancient Sparta prided itself on producing ultimately healthy and fit citizens.

- Throughout history, there has always been a popular philosophy about "wellness" even if it wasn't called by that name.

✔ What have some of these philosophies been throughout history?

2) Divide class into groups of 4–5 students.

3) Assign each group one of the following eras to research:

©1994 Whole Person Press 210 W Michigan Duluth MN 55802   (800) 247-6789

Early Greece and Rome   **Renaissance**
Colonial America   **The nineteenth century**
1920–1930   **1940–1950**
1960–1970   **1980–1990**
Projections for the future

4) Instruct students to find out as much as they can about attitudes regarding health and wellness for their time period.

5) The following are ideas you may want them to pursue in their research:

- Physical wellness: examine fitness, nutrition, health, disease, or the health care system and determine what aspects have changed.

- Mental wellness: examine self-esteem/self-worth and determine what aspects have changed

- Spiritual wellness: determine how its focus has changed

- Environmental wellness: examine how the focus on pollution, conservation, or care of the environment has changed.

- Additional interest areas might include women's wellness/children's wellness.

- The advancements in medical technology and health care.

- The effects of the farm-to-city movement.

6) When completed, have groups report their findings back to the class.

7) Make a large chart on the blackboard to record the major changes in each area of wellness as reported by the groups.

8) Use the following questions as discussion starters:

✔ What are the major changes we have seen in the philosophy of health and wellness?

✔ Has the basic philosophy changed over the years?

✔ What is the most surprising thing you learned?

✔ What is the most disturbing thing you learned?

✔ Where are we going from here?

✔ Do you think that "wellness" will continue to be a major philosophy of health and self-care?

✔ What do you think the "next wave" will be?

✔ What part will technology play in future wellness?

14 YESTERDAY, TODAY, & TOMORROW

This activity gives students the chance to look at the results of positive and negative lifestyle choices that begin in childhood and follow us into our adult lives.

GOALS

Trace positive and negative lifestyles and their effects on the individual from childhood through adulthood.

Emphasize the importance of making positive choices about our lives as early as possible to have the greatest chance of abundant living.

TIME FRAME

45–50 minutes

AGE GROUP

Upper elementary through senior high

MATERIALS

None.

PROCESS

1) Begin with a discussion using the following points:

   ● What we do today—how we care for ourselves—will continue to be with us in years to come.

   ● Many of our dis-eases in this society begin in childhood before we even have much of a say in our own health.

   ● Many of the habits involving your nutrition, fitness, and self-care you have today had their beginnings when you were a small child, before you had very much to say about your own care, and before you had the knowledge to make considered, informed choices.

   ● If you look at how your habits may have begun, you can help yourselves see ways in which you can turn them around while you are still young and have the opportunity for a full, rich, long, and healthy life.

- This activity will test your thinking power and your knowledge about habits, lifestyle behaviors, risk factors, and the resulting physical and emotional conditions.

2) Divide the class into groups of 4–6 students each.

3) Give each group a card with a description of a child on it. See the examples on page 37 or make up your own to fit the purposes of your class session.

☞ *Encourage students to consider all sides of their child's situation, both positive and negative, and to look at alternatives to possible obvious consequences.*

4) Give each group about ten minutes to brainstorm the results of this child's behavior and to describe in detail how those results will follow him or her throughout his or her life.

5) Reconvene the groups and have each group describe their child and the conclusions they reached concerning this child's habits and wellness prospects.

6) After all teams have presented their conclusion, use the following for discussion questions:

✔ Do you see yourself in any of these scenarios?

✔ Do you see anyone in your family or a friend in any of these?

✔ Have you considered the long-term results of the habits you are practicing?

✔ Does it matter to you or do you think you have plenty of time to make changes before the negative consequences catch up with you?

✔ Is it okay to wait until you are older to make changes in your behavior?

WELLNESS SCENARIOS

Use these scenarios or make up some of your own.

■ Child, seven years old. Watches television from 3:30 p.m. until bedtime and all day on Saturday. Eats snacks while in front of the TV set.

What will he be like at 15? 25? 45? 70? What will the consequences of his behavior be at each of these ages?

■ Child, seven years old. Refuses to eat vegetables. Screams for candy and soda. To pacify him and keep peace, his parents give in.

What could he be like at 15? 25? 45? 70? What are the long-term consequences of his habits? Which parts of his life will be affected at each of these ages?

■ Child, seven years old. Parents refuse to buy candy and cookies. She is only allowed to watch 1 hour of TV a day.

What will she possibly be like at 15? 25? 45? 70? What will be the long-term consequences of her behavior? How will her life be affected at each of these ages?

■ Child, ten years old. Sneaks a cigarette with his friends behind the school several afternoons a week.

What will he possibly be like at 15? 25? 45? 70? What are the long-term consequences of his behavior? How will his life be affected at each of these ages?

■ Child, eight years old, is subjected to constant fighting at home. She has to yell to be heard, can't get her homework done because of the turmoil.

What will she possible be like at 15? 25? 45? 70? What are the long-term consequences of this situation? How will her life be affected at each of these ages?

■ Child, ten years old. Both parents are outdoors people, but this child prefers to read and work on his computer. His parents insist he accompany them on all hikes and camping trips. They say it will be better for him than sitting at home in front of the computer.

What will he possibly be like at 15? 25? 45? 70? What are the long-term consequences of his situation? How will he be affected at each of these ages?

■ Child, eight years old. Parents adore her, but don't spoil her. She has rules to follow. She is given responsibilities and is held accountable for them. If she does not follow through, she suffers the consequences of those behaviors and has privileges removed.

What will she possibly be like at 15? 25? 45? 70? What are the long-term consequences of her situation? How will her life be affected at each of these ages?

©1994 Whole Person Press 210 W Michigan Duluth MN 55802   (800) 247-6789

15 FLYING HIGH

This fun activity for younger children helps celebrate all the great things they are already doing to have a wellness-oriented life.

GOALS

Help students celebrate themselves.

Create a visual reminder of all the positive wellness-oriented things they are already doing for themselves.

TIME FRAME

20 minutes

AGE GROUP

Younger elementary but can be adapted for any age

MATERIALS NEEDED

Flying High With Wellness worksheets: one large worksheet for class presentation; individual worksheets for each student.

PROCESS

1) Use the following points in a discussion:

   ● Wellness isn't just a bunch of rules telling us what we should and shouldn't do.

   ● Wellness is also taking a look at who we are and celebrating all the good things we already do for ourselves.

   ● Looking at how great we are should make us feel so high that we feel like a kite just floating up there in the air, happy and proud to be who we are.

   ● I think we have a terrific class and I think we are doing many wonderful things that show we are working on getting *better and better* in our lives.

2) Show the **Flying High With Wellness** worksheet.

3) Discuss the four major areas of wellness designated by the worksheet:

Physical wellness
Emotional wellness
Intellectual wellness
Environmental wellness

4) Discuss with the children the things they are doing as a class that helps all of them live a better life.

- **Physical**—we go outside and run each day as a class; we learn about nutrition in health class so we can eat better.

- **Emotional**—we learn how to handle our anger in constructive ways; we have a special buddy for the day to share our feelings with.

- **Intellectual**—we learned new math facts today.

- **Environmental**—we recycle our paper from class.

5) As children offer suggestions of the things they are doing as a class to live a wellness-oriented life, discuss which area of wellness that suggestion might apply to and write it in that area of the kite.

➤ Suggestions:

➣ Color the four areas of the kite four different colors, a different color for each area of wellness.

➣ Label each area.

➣ Attach a long tail string to the kite.

➣ Make tail pieces from strips of construction paper in corresponding colors to the four sections.

➣ Make the tail pieces in the shape of a bow:

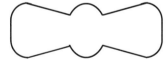

➣ As children suggest wellness habits they have developed as a class, write them on the tail piece that corresponds with the appropriate areas of wellness.

➣ Attach pieces to tail string with tape.

6) Use the following for class discussion:

✔ Are any areas under-represented?

✔ What does this tell you about what we need to work on to get even better?

©1994 Whole Person Press 210 W Michigan Duluth MN 55802   (800) 247-6789

✔ What is our strongest area?

7) After completing the classroom chart, distribute individual **Flying High With Wellness** worksheets to the children.

8) Use the following points for introduction:

   ● You know, we can't fly high as a class unless each one of us takes very good care of ourselves.

   ● What things do you do on a daily basis that helps you be a really well person?

9) Go around the class and have each child give an example of something he or she does on a daily basis that helps him "fly high with wellness," i.e., "I brush my teeth every morning before I come to school."

10) Have the child tell you which area of wellness that habit fits into.

11) Then ask everyone in the class who has that same positive habit to raise his or her hand.

12) The children can write the habits they possess in the appropriate area of the kite, or for younger children, they can add stripes of color in each area of the kite for the habits they possess.

13) Instruct children who don't have that habit yet, but think it would be a good idea, to write it on the bottom of their worksheets as a reminder of something they would like to do for themselves.

14) Continue to go around the class until everyone has had the opportunity to share.

15) Use the following points for discussion:

   ✔ What are the strongest areas of wellness in this class?

   ✔ What is the weakest area?

   ✔ How do you feel about the habits you have already developed?

   ✔ What is one habit you would like to develop that will help you stay strong and well?

FLYING HIGH WITH WELLNESS

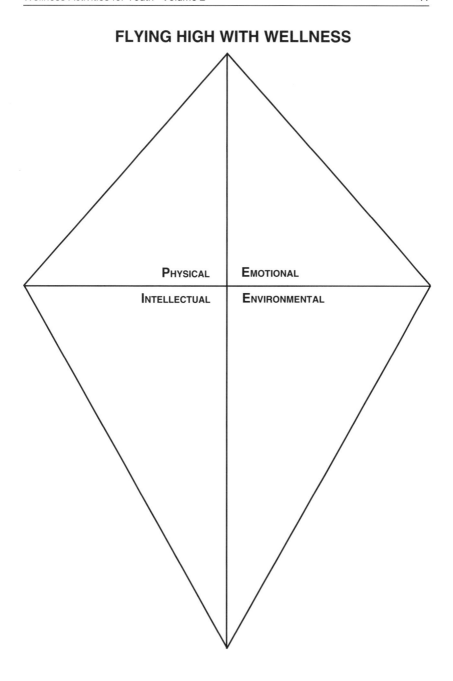

PHYSICAL

EMOTIONAL

INTELLECTUAL

ENVIRONMENTAL

16 ROLLING ALONG

This activity offers a visual model of wellness and helps students appreciate that the more intricate their identity—the more things they have to identify themselves by—the more positive a life they will lead.

GOALS

Provide a visual model for wellness.

Understand that the more qualities we can use to identify ourselves—the more varied our lives— the greater our chance for balance and a healthy self-esteem.

Understand that self-responsibility and self-esteem are at the heart of the wellness lifestyle.

TIME FRAME

45–50 minutes

AGE GROUP

Upper elementary through senior high

MATERIALS NEEDED

Large diagram of bicycle wheel on blackboard; **Bicycle Wheel** worksheet for each student.

PROCESS

l) Begin with the following points for discussion:

- Sometimes it's difficult to understand wellness and how it fits into our lives.

- One of the best ways of visualizing it is to look at a bicycle wheel. A bicycle wheel consists of a central hub from which many spokes extend. These spokes support the shape of the wheel and the length of the spokes determine the size of the wheel.

- The more spokes there are in a bicycle wheel, the more support the wheel has.

- And so it is with our lives. The more parts there are to each of us—the more varied our lives—the better chance we have to lead a balanced life and the less chance we have for serious depression.

- Remember the hub that holds the wheel together? This hub represents self-responsibility in the wellness lifestyle. When you take on the goal of self-responsibility you take on the challenge of holding all of your varied "spokes" together in a working whole.

- But the most important thing to the inner construction of the wheel is the little nut and bolt assembly that holds the hub and spokes together and keeps them tight. The nut and bolt set represents self-esteem. If you like yourself and feel worthwhile, taking care of yourself is easy. Liking one's self is the crucial part of a wellness lifestyle. When you care for yourself as the person you are, you take on self-responsibility and seek out a variety of interests, creating a large number of "spokes" in your wheel. A wheel with only a few spokes soon wears out. A person with only a limited number of interests soon becomes bored and depressed and is easily influenced by others.

- Studies have shown that the more intricate your view of yourself, the more resistant you are to the negative effects of stress. That means, the more spokes you have in your wheel, the more likely you are to live a positive life with less chance of stress and depression becoming a chronic problem.

- A group of students were given 33 cards, each listing a feature—such as outgoing, affectionate or lazy—as descriptors. They were asked to sort the card into as many piles as they thought represented aspects of themselves.

  Those students who had a higher self-complexity score—more aspects or ways in which they saw themselves—were those less likely to become depressed and report physical ailments such as flu, back problems, headache, and menstrual cramps when stressed.

- Why does this work? A stressful event begins causing trouble by infiltrating a person's most important self aspects. A tennis player who has just lost an important match is likely to feel dejected. These negative feelings are part of his "tennis player self." This feeling, however, shouldn't spill over into other parts of his life if he has other characteristics by which to identify himself.

● How many spokes do you have in your wheel? How many parts of you are there? Are you JUST an athlete? Do you live and breathe only sports? Are you JUST a student? Do you spend all your time studying with no other outlets for your creativity or energy? Are you JUST a party animal? Do you mark time waiting for the next party, while your school work goes down the drain? Remember, the fewer the spokes, the more limited your Self, the more susceptible you are to stress, peer pressure, and depression.

2) Distribute **Bicycle Wheel** worksheets to each student.

3) Use the following instructions for completing the worksheets:

➤ Draw and label as many spokes as apply to you within each of the areas of wellness on the wheel.

➤ The spokes should represent descriptions of who you are and what you like to do in your life.

➤ Some examples might be the following:

➤ Basketball player—physical

➤ Party animal—social

➤ Great at math—intellectual

➤ Like to laugh—emotional

➤ Have lots of friends—social

➤ Go to church every Sunday—spiritual

➤ The spokes should represent not just personal characteristics but should represent those characteristics that you actually put time and effort into being. Just SAYING you are something doesn't cut it; you must BE it.

➤ Once you have completed your wheel, darken those spokes that are most important to you.

4) Use the following points for follow-up discussion:

✔ Which part of your wheel had the most spokes?

✔ Do you have a balanced approach to your life?

✔ Is any area really over-represented? Under-represented?

THE BICYCLE WHEEL

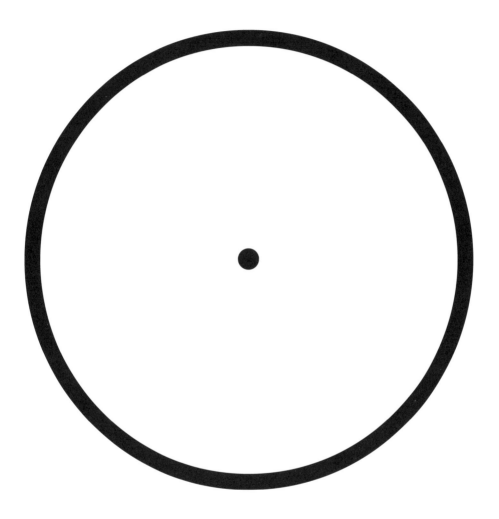

17 WELLNESS JOURNAL

This journaling experience helps students identify the ways they care for themselves daily in each of the major wellness areas.

GOALS

Journal daily self-care experiences.

Observe whether we are living balanced lives.

Become aware of the areas in our lives that need increased self-care.

TIME FRAME

Several weeks

AGE GROUP

Upper elementary through senior high

MATERIALS NEEDED

Enough **Wellness Journal** worksheets for each student to use over two weeks.

PROCESS

1) Begin by asking the students the following questions:

   ✔ What do you do for yourself each day that helps create a wellness lifestyle for yourself?

   ✔ Do you do things for yourself in each of the areas of wellness—physical, mental/emotional, social, intellectual, spiritual, environmental?

   ✔ Do you save certain areas of wellness for only one day of the week-i.e., church on Sunday or only one day of aerobics a week—or do you do a little something for yourself each day of the week in each area?

2) Instruct students in the journaling process.

   ➤ Each day for two weeks, I want you to spend a little time assessing what you have done for yourself during that day in each of the areas of wellness.

➤ Use the journal pages provided to briefly record the things you did for yourself that day in each of the areas of wellness.

☞ *You could also have them create a journal of their own.*

➤ If you can't think of anything for one particular area, leave it blank, and try to concentrate on doing something for yourself in that area during the next day.

➤ Pay attention to the balance you have in your life each day.

➤ Remember, too, that many things can be included in your journal. Some are obvious, and some may be less obvious, but just as important.

3) Discuss with students items that could go in each area of wellness. Write the list on the board and encourage students to make notes for themselves to help them in their journaling process. The following is a brief list to help you along. Add your own to the list.

Physical: Exercise; nutrition; doctor/dental visit; avoiding alcohol/tobacco; rest.

Mental/Emotional: Self esteem enhancement; spending time thinking and evaluating; crying; laughing; spending time alone to think.

Social: Spending time with friends; clubs; family time; writing letters; volunteering.

Intellectual: Reading voluntarily; visiting museum; concert; theater; homework; investing in your schoolwork.

Spiritual: Prayer; meditation; listening to music; attending church or synagogue; time alone to center.

Environmental: Recycling; helping to clean up around home/community; noise pollution awareness (loud stereos, etc.); hiking; community projects.

☞ *Some items may fit in more than one category.*

4) Have students write in their journals for a two week period.

5) Check with them periodically throughout the process for any questions or problems they may be having.

6) At the completion of the journaling time, use the following questions for follow-up:

✔ Did you find it easy or difficult to complete this project? Why?

✔ What did you find out about yourself?

✔ Are you more or less balanced in your lifestyle than you thought you were?

✔ What was your biggest surprise?

✔ Are there any areas of your life that particularly need attention?

✔ Are you over-balanced in any areas?

7) Encourage students to continue with their journal as a personal project.

TRAINER'S NOTES

WELLNESS JOURNAL

Spend a few quiet moments each day and record what you did for yourself that day in each of the following areas of wellness.

Physical

Mental/Emotional

Spiritual

Intellectual

Environmental

18 WELL, WELL, WELL

Students create a project that looks at the qualities of a well person.

GOALS

Help younger students identify the characteristics of positive and negative lifestyles.

Emphasize that wellness goes beyond a health-based philosophy.

TIME FRAME

1 hour

AGE GROUP

Elementary

MATERIALS NEEDED

Old magazines; tape or glue and scissors; large sheet of backing paper for each group of 4–5 students.

PROCESS

1) Begin with background discussion:

- The word "wellness" can sometimes be confusing. What do you think it means?

- Sometimes people think that "wellness" means just not being sick. If I come to school and I feel OK, then I must be "well," they think.

- But there is more to it than that. Wellness means being healthy in our bodies, our thought, AND our feelings.

- I'll bet each of you can remember having had a day when you were physically healthy—you weren't sick—but you were feeling so sad or mad that you had a really rotten day.

- You may have been "healthy" but you were having an "un-well" day because your feelings were putting your day out of balance.

- Everyone has days like that. Wellness means we look at our lives and pay attention to all the things we can do to have the very best lives we can and to do those things regularly.

- It doesn't mean we will always be happy or healthy, but it does mean we make choices that will help us stay as happy and as healthy as we can be.

- Wellness doesn't just include physical health, like eating good food and taking a bath. It includes many other areas of our lives as well.

2) Make a list on the board and use the following explanatory information to help the students understand the various areas of wellness:

   1. PHYSICAL—brushing teeth, exercise, doctor/dental visits, bathing, avoiding alcohol, drugs, and tobacco, etc.

   - Wellness means doing all those things to help our bodies stay strong and healthy.

   2. EMOTIONAL—feelings; it's okay to be mad; dealing with our feelings in appropriate ways.

   - Wellness means that we look at all of our feelings—good/bad, happy/sad and realize they are all okay. It's not our feelings that get us into trouble. It is often what we DO with our feelings that causes us trouble.

   ✔ Are well people always happy? Why or why not?

   3. SOCIAL—having friends.

   - Wellness means getting along with other people. It means being able to see that other people have value.

   ✔ Are well people friends with everyone?

   ✔ Is it okay not to have *everyone* as your "best friend?"

   4. MENTAL—self esteem.

   - Wellness means liking yourself, knowing that you are a one-of-a-kind, never-to-be-repeated person. When we like ourselves then we WANT to take care of ourselves.

   5. INTELLECTUAL—school work.

   - Wellness means using your mind. It means you realize that you are a truly smart person who can learn and WANTS to learn because you want to grow up to be able to think for yourself.

      ☞ *You can include other areas in your explanation if you like, i.e., environmental, spiritual, etc. Use as few or as many as your children are able to understand.*

3) Divide the class into small groups of 4–5 students.

4) Distribute materials.

5) Instruct students to look through the magazines and find pictures that represent what they think a "well" person looks like, uses, feels like, etc., including words and phrases they think describe a well person.

6) Instruct them to draw a line down the center of their backing paper. On one side of the paper, they will paste pictures of positive wellness pictures, words and phrases; on the other side they will paste pictures of "un-well" habits, words, etc. (This should take about 20–25 minutes.)

7) Reconvene for discussion. Have each group share their collage with the rest of the class, explaining their choices for well *vs.* unwell lifestyle habits.

8) Use the following points for discussion:

✔ What kinds of pictures do we associate with wellness?

✔ Were all the areas of wellness represented on your collage?

✔ Which areas were most represented?

✔ Which were least represented?

✔ If someone did/used everything you included on your positive side, would they be a well person?

LIFE STAGES

19 LIFELINE TO WELLNESS (p 54)

This activity helps students see that everyone has experienced both the good times and the not-so-good times in their lives, and emphasizes that it is up to us to use the not-so-good times as challenges for making things better for ourselves in the future.
(1–2 class periods)

20 THE WORLD'S A-CHANGING (p 57)

Students examine changes in their lives and analyze how they have handled the changes as well as how a wellness lifestyle can help with future changes. (2 class periods)

21 WHEN I BECOME A PARENT (p 59)

Students look at what they think they will be like as parents and explore their feelings about what it means to be a parent.
(20–30 minutes)

22 MIRROR, MIRROR (p 63)

In this visualization activity, students try to see themselves as they age.
(1 or more class periods)

23 WHAT ABOUT DEATH? (p 67)

Children receive input from parents or other significant adults about their ideas and attitudes about death.
(requires at home and class time)

24 I GREW AND I GREW AND . . . (p 69)

Looking at how we change is an exciting process for upper elementary children. This activity encourages the celebration of those changes in themselves and others. (several days)

25 I AM . . . (p 72)

This highly interactive activity helps students identify the main contributors to their self-esteem as well as giving them the chance to affirm each other with positive feedback. (45–50 minutes)

26 WHO AM I? (p 76)

This activity helps students identify twenty of their lifestyle characteristics and helps them examine those that contribute to or detract from their personal wellness.
(1–2 class periods)

19 LIFELINE TO WELLNESS

This activity helps students see that everyone has experienced both the good times and the not-so-good times in their lives, and emphasizes that it is up to us to use the not-so-good times as challenges for making things better for ourselves in the future.

GOALS

Demonstrate that we all have both good and troubling times in our lives.

Emphasize that "bad things" don't have to keep us down but can be turned into challenges for future achievement.

TIME FRAME

1–2 class periods

AGE GROUP

Upper elementary through senior high

MATERIALS NEEDED

Three legal size (8 ½" x 14") sheets of paper for each student.

PROCESS

1) Begin with the following discussion points:

- We have all had times in our lives when things coast along and we feel great.

- And, we have all had times when nothing seems to go right, when everything seems to conspire against us to make us miserable.

- Sometimes it seems as if we are the only ones who have ever suffered through bad, depressing times.

- Try to think of a time when something happen to you that, at the time, seemed like a negative event, which in the end, turned out to be something positive.

2) Distribute three blank 8 ½" x 14" sheets of paper to each student.

3) Instruct students as follows:

☞ *You may wish to illustrate your instructions by drawing your own lifeline or that of some fictional character the entire class is familiar with.*

➤ Place paper horizontally.

➤ Draw a line that represents your life's ups and downs beginning at the left end of the paper and continuing across the paper until you get to the place you are right now in your life. If something really great happened to you (you learned to walk) obviously your lifeline would take a leap upward.

➤ If something happened to you that was a real downer, your lifeline will dip.

➤ If several things happened in succession, either good or bad, you can illustrate by successive leaps or dips.

➤ As you leap or dip, illustrate the age at which this happened and the event that happened. Include everything, no matter how insignificant it may seem. Getting a pet or losing a pet are critical events in a child's life. Getting your first good report card or getting your first "D" in math are also critical events.

➤ When you have gotten all the way to where you are now, stop and take a look at your lifeline. Are there more ups than downs? Downs than ups? Has your attitude about life in general been affected by the number of ups and downs you have had so far in your life? Have you risen above the negative things that have happened to you or do they still affect the way you see things?

➤ Remember that whatever happened to you in the past is IN THE PAST and is not affecting you unless you choose to let it.

4) Divide students into groups of 3–4 to share their lifelines.

5) After sharing, have students trace their lifelines onto the second sheet of paper without labeling or signing them.

6) Collect all time lines and display around the classroom as a visual representation of the ups and downs that all of us have experienced.

7) Use the anonymous tracings for the following discussion questions:

✔ If you were this person, with all the disappointments he/she has had in life, what would you say to this person about his or her attitude toward life? What recommendations would you give them about turning the negatives into positives?

©1994 Whole Person Press 210 W Michigan Duluth MN 55802   (800) 247-6789

✔ If you were this person with all these good things happening, what kind of person do you think you might be? What kind of attitude might you have toward life?

● Remember that having good things happen to us does not necessarily mean that we will have a positive attitude about life. Some people feel miserable in spite of the good things, and some people rise above all the negatives in their lives and are able to feel really good about themselves.

8) For the second part of this activity, instruct students to imagine the years they have ahead and create a time line based on how they think their lives will go.

9) Use the third sheet of paper to draw a time line based on these expectations. Use the following questions to help them along:

✔ What kinds of ups and downs can you expect?

✔ Do you think you will have more ups than downs? Downs than ups?

10) Divide students into small groups to discuss their feelings about the future or use as class discussion.

11) Ask students what things they can do now that will help make their futures more positive.

☞ *This activity can be a good starting place for a discussion on the various areas of wellness.*

20 THE WORLD'S A-CHANGING

Students examine changes in their lives and analyze how they have handled the changes as well as how a wellness lifestyle can help with future changes.

GOALS

Recognize change as a normal and necessary part of life.

Recognize that growth involves change.

Look at developing skills to deal with the stress of change.

TIME FRAME

45–60 minutes

AGE GROUP

Upper elementary through junior high

MATERIALS NEEDED

A sheet of notebook paper for each student.

PROCESS

1) Begin by presenting the following points for discussion:

- We experience changes in our lives from birth to death.

- Sometimes the changes are small and insignificant to us; other times they are enormous and earth shattering.

- We can feel differently about changes at different ages.

- Sometimes we like changes; other times we hate changes and are afraid of them.

- Part of being a well person is recognizing change as a necessary and inevitable part of life and developing skills that allow us to accept change without undue stress.

2) Instruct students to try to remember the major changes that occurred at various times in their lives: age 2, 5, 7, 9, 11, etc.

3) On a clean sheet of paper, have the students construct a change section for each age as follows:

➤ At top of page, write, "Age 2."

➤ Underneath, write "Major Changes."

➤ List the major changes you can remember or can imagine happened when you were two years old.

➤ Beside each, write, "How I Handled Those Changes."

➤ Record, to the best of their memory or imagination, how you think you may have handled the many changes that occured when you were a two-year-old, for example:

Age 2:

Major Changes	How I Handled Those Changes
My brother was born	*Got jealous and cried*
Went from a crib to a bed	*Enjoyed my new freedom*
Stopped taking a bottle	*Liked being a "big boy"*

4) Repeat the process for ages 5, 7, 9, 11, etc. When students reach their current age, have them complete the process with "Changes that a Seventh Grade student might experience," and "how I will handle those changes."

5) After completion of all ages, discuss the various ages and changes as a group.

6) Make a list of the following words on the board and ask students to choose those that best describe the changes they have experienced:

few	**many**	**too many**	**not enough**
exciting	**confusing**	**great**	**scary**
necessary	**not often**	**recent**	**years ago**
pleasant	**sickening**	**gross**	**OK**
weird	**mind blowing**	**fun**	**uncomfortable**

7) Use the following points for discussion:

✔ Has your way of reacting to and handling change remained the same over the years, or has it changed? How?

✔ Do changes usually affect you in a positive or negative way? What have you learned from the changes in your life?

✔ Can a wellness lifestyle help with the changes you will experience in the next several years? How?

✔ What is the major change you think you will confront in the next year? Five years? Ten years?

21 WHEN I BECOME A PARENT

Students look at what they think they will be like as parents and explore their feelings about what it means to be a parent.

GOALS

Examine student values about parenting.

TIME FRAME

20–30 minutes

AGE GROUP

Upper elementary through senior high

MATERIALS NEEDED

A **Parenting** worksheet for each student.

PROCESS

1) Begin with the following warm-up discussion:

- Parenting is the world's most difficult profession. It is something we are not trained for and yet are expected to carry out successfully.

  ✔ How many of you think your parents have done a pretty good job with you? How?

  ✔ What are some gripes that young people often have about their parents? Why do they feel this way?

  ✔ Will you be different with your own kids? How?

  ✔ What kind of parent do you think you will be?

  ✔ What will you do differently than your parents have done with you?

  ✔ What things will you do the same as your parents have done with you?

- You may find this difficult to believe, but no matter what you may think of your parents, you will probably parent your children in much the same way that you are being parented because the only things you know about parenting is what your parents have taught you by the way they have raised you.

☞ *You will get a lot of groans and denials. It is important that young people understand that if there is something going on in the home that is uncomfortable or unpleasant, those things are quite likely to be repeated unless they decide to change them with their own children, because it is what has been models for them.*

2) Distribute **Parenting** worksheets to each student.

3) Instruct students to complete worksheets. Allow 10–15 minutes for completion.

4) When completed, share the results as a group.

5) Lead a discussion, making the following points:

- There is no such thing as a perfect parent.

- We will parent based on how we were parented.

- It is normal for young people to pull away from their parents, but it is important to remember that we all come back to those values that have been modeled for us.

- We can change negative parent role modeling if we choose to.

WHEN I BECOME A PARENT

When you have children of your own...

1. What rules would you have for a five-year-old?

    a.

    b.

    c.

    Are these the same rules your parents had for you?

2. What rules would you have for a ten-year-old?

    a.

    b.

    c.

    Are these the same rules you parents had for you?

3. What would you tell your kids about drugs? Is this the same thing your parents have told you?

4. What things would you allow your children to do that you were not allowed to do? Why?

5. What things would you not allow your kids to do that you were allowed to do? Why?

6. What would you never do to your children that your parents have done with you?

    a.

    b.

    c.

7. What would you never say to your children that your parents have said to you?

   a.

   b.

   c.

8. How will your children be different from you?

9. How will your children be the same as you?

10. What rules will you have for your children when they are teenagers?

   a.

   b.

   c.

11. Suppose your teen called home drunk one night. What would you do? What would your parents do?

12. What will you tell your teen about birth control? What have you been told?

13. What will you do if one of your teens gets into trouble? What would your parents do?

14. Suppose your children play music, wear clothes or have friends you don't approve of. What will you do?

22 MIRROR, MIRROR

In this visualization activity, students try to see themselves as they age.

GOALS

Experience a mental image of one's own aging and the changes that will occur with this process.

Promote inter-generational understanding.

Examine the aging process as a normal life process.

TIME FRAME

One class period or more if needed

AGE GROUP

Junior and senior high school

MATERIALS

None.

PROCESS

1) Familiarize yourself thoroughly with this activity before using it in class. If possible, have someone read the script and guide you through the process so that you understand both what is being done in this activity as well as your own feelings about the activity.

2) Practice reading the script aloud before you present it in class. Develop a smooth, slow pace and remember to pause at the end of each sentence. Speak in a gentle but encouraging voice that is loud enough to be heard clearly.

3) Reading the **Mirror, Mirror on the Wall** script, lead the class in the imagery activity in a comfortable, quiet, darkened room.

4) After you have finished with the activity, use the following questions for discussion:

   ✔ What was your image of being 10?

   ✔ What was your image of being 40? How did you feel about that?

   ✔ What did you base your image on?

✔ Did you use anyone in your life as the basis for your image?

✔ What was your image of being 70?

✔ What did you base your image on?

✔ Did you use anyone in your life as the basis for your image?

✔ What do you think the hardest thing about being 10 was?

✔ What was the easiest? Best?

✔ What do you think the most difficult thing about being 40 will be?

✔ What will be the easiest? Best?

✔ What do you think the most difficult thing about being 70 will be?

✔ What will be the easiest? Best?

✔ How do you think you will be different at all these ages?

✔ How do you think you will remain the same?

✔ Will it be fun being 40? 70?

✔ What will you like? What will you NOT like?

✔ How many people do you know who are 70?

✔ What do you like and/or respect about these people?

✔ What do you not like and/or feel sorry about people this age?

✔ What do you fear about people this age?

✔ What was your favorite age during this exercise?

✔ As you thought about people of generations other than your own, what new perspectives did you gain?

✔ Did any images surprise or concern you?

✔ How did you feel about this activity?

✔ Did you get any different insights about your life from this activity?

MIRROR, MIRROR ON THE WALL Script

Get into a comfortable position.

Take a deep breath and let it go. When you are ready, close your eyes. If at any time during this activity you feel uncomfortable, just open your eyes and do the activity with your eyes open, or just wait quietly for the rest of us to finish.

Now take a moment to pay attention to your breathing. Notice how the air comes into your body, where it goes and how it feels. Notice as you breathe out, how the air leaves your body and how that feels. As you're noticing this, let your body relax and let your mind feel calm and alert.

Now imagine a mirror. Let it be a full-length mirror. Notice whether it is on a stand or on a wall. Let it have a frame. Notice the frame, its color, its texture.

Now see yourself standing in front of the mirror and looking into it and seeing your own image. As you see your reflection in the mirror, notice yourself. Notice what you are wearing, how you're standing, how your face looks.

Now let this become a very special mirror, one that can show your image, not just in the present, but in many different times of your life. Let the image you have of yourself fade now and let it be replaced by an image of you at about ten years old. What are you wearing? How does your hair look? What does your face look like? Your teeth? Let that ten-year-old greet you. What do you sound like. What does your smile look like? Imagine your ten-year-old doing something he or she likes to do. What is it?

Now let an older person be with your ten-year-old. It might be a grandparent or older friend of the family. Watch these two people together. Notice how they feel about each other. Now let that image fade away.

Now let the mirror show you another image of yourself. Now you are about forty years old. Begin by just letting the image appear. What kind of clothes are you wearing? What does your face look like? Eyes? Hairstyle? Get a good sense of who you are at this stage.

What is important to you at this age? How do you feel about this forty-year-old person?

Now watch this forty-year-old you doing something with a ten-year-old. Who is this child? What are you doing with the child? How do you feel about being with this child? Watch them for a moment and then let the ten-year-old go.

©1994 Whole Person Press 210 W Michigan Duluth MN 55802   (800) 247-6789

Imagine the forty-year-old being joined by a person about seventy. How do they greet each other? What is their relationship? Watch them together. How do you, the forty-year-old, feel about this older person? Let both images fade into the mirror.

Now let an image of you appear again. This time let yourself be 70 years old. Take a moment to get used to this image of you. What are you doing? What does your face look like? Your eyes? Your hairstyle? Your body? How do you feel about being this person? Now imagine this seventy-year-old you in the place where you live. Let yourself become that person for a few moments. Look around that place where you live. Is it a house? An apartment? A retirement community? A nursing home? Notice your surroundings. Notice the colors, sounds and smells that surround you. Does anyone else live with you?

Now imagine a young person coming to visit you. Let it be someone about ten years old. Notice how you feel about being with that person. Do you enjoy it? What do you like to do together? What is the biggest difficulty in your relationship with this person? Who is this person?

Spend some time with this person. Now say good-bye to that ten-year-old.

Imagine someone else visiting you—someone about 40 years old. Get an image of that person. Again, notice how you feel about being with him or her. What do you like about that person? What is your biggest problem with this person? Imagine yourself having a conversation. What are you talking about? Now say good-bye to this person and let him or her go.

Take a moment for yourself. Feel yourself as that seventy-year-old person. Get a sense of how you like to spend your time when you are alone. What do you like to do? What do you like about your life? What do you NOT like about your life? Are there things that worry you? If you had one wish, what would it be?

Now let that seventy-year-old person be an image in the mirror with you watching. As you do that, let the image fade and let it be replaced by an image of yourself as you are now. What did you learn from this journey through time with yourself? What do you like about your life so far? Where do you see yourself going? What age in your life do you think will be your most favorite? Think about the other people in your life right now who are different ages and generations.

Begin to bring your attention back to the room where we are now. Notice your breathing. Notice the place where you are sitting or lying. Notice the other people around you. When you are ready, slowly open your eyes and be back in the moment.

23 WHAT ABOUT DEATH?

Children receive input from parents or other significant adults about their ideas and attitudes about death.

GOALS

Examining attitudes and beliefs about death and dying.

Building communication about death between parents and children.

TIME FRAME

At-home time to complete activity. Classroom discussion time.

AGE GROUP

Upper elementary through junior high

MATERIALS NEEDED

Letter for parents; *The Fall of Freddy the Leaf* by Leo Buscaglia (this wonderful, very short book is published by Slack, Inc. and available in most bookstores).

> ☞ *This exercise concerns a topic that is both very sensitive and very important. Take time and care to adapt it appropriately for your group.*

PROCESS

1) Begin by presenting the following points as an introduction:

   ● Part of learning to live well is to understand that death is part of life.

   ● Your chances of dying are the same as they have always been— 100%!

   ● No matter how well and healthy we are, we will all die one of these days.

2) Continue by asking the following questions for discussion:

   ✔ What is your biggest fear about death?

   ✔ What are some questions you have about death and dying?

☞ *You may want to have children write down and place in a question box any questions they have about death. Spend a class period answering their questions.*

✔ What are your experiences with death?

✔ How does it feel when we lose someone or something we care about?

3) Have children go home and ask their parents what they would like them to know about death.

4) Send a note home with your students asking parents or grandparents to write down what they would like their child to know about death in the form of a letter to their child.

5) Instruct students to bring these papers back to class to be shared with the group.

☞ *If students don't bring letters back, don't press. The children will still benefit from hearing some of the things that other parents have written.*

Also, make it okay not to share if the child does not care to.

6) Encourage students to keep these letters in a special place where they won't lose them so that they will have these letters in the future.

7) Use the following as questions for discussion after sharing:

✔ How did these letters make you feel?

✔ What do you think is the main message that most of our parents/ grandparents want us to know about death?

✔ Does talking about death make it any less frightening or confusing?

8) Read "The Fall of Freddy the Leaf" by Leo Buscaglia as a nice ending to this class.

9) After reading, use the following questions to initiate a discussion.

✔ What does this story try to tell us about death?

✔ What was Freddy most afraid of?

✔ Why?

✔ What did he find out at the end of his life?

✔ What did Daniel help him understand?

24 I GREW AND I GREW AND...

Looking at how we change is an exciting process for upper elementary children. This activity encourages the celebration of those changes in themselves and others.

GOALS

Look at growth and change in a positive way.

Celebrate our changes with others and help them celebrate their changes.

Involve families in helping the child acknowledge and celebrate growing up.

TIME FRAME

This project will take several days for the child to complete at home. Sharing of the projects should be done a few at a time during class so that each child has time to share.

AGE GROUP

Upper elementary

MATERIALS NEEDED

I Was Born . . . and I Grew and I Grew and I Grew worksheet for each child.

> ☞ *You will want to duplicate the worksheets on 11" x 17" sheets of paper to allow enough space for photographs that will be attached.*

PROCESS

1) Distribute worksheets to each student.

2) Instruct them to take the sheets home and, with the help of their families, attach pictures that illustrate how they grew and grew and grew.

3) Send a note home to parents telling them about the project and assuring them that pictures will be safe in your classroom and will be returned.

4) At the bottom of the page, have the child ask a parent or grandparent to write how that person feels about this child.

5) Let each child share his or her completed growth record with the rest of the class, noting when pictures were taken, how old she or he was at the time, and reading what the parent or other relative had to say about the child.

☞ *This is an especially effective project when used in conjunction with family life programs.*

6) Use the following points for discussion during the sharing process:

✔ What kinds of changes has everyone gone through?

✔ Looking at the pictures of this child with her family, what similarities can you notice?

✔ What are the major changes you notice from babyhood to childhood? From kindergarten to middle elementary?

TRAINER'S NOTES

I WAS BORN . . . AND I GREW, AND I GREW, AND I GREW

I WAS BORN   Name_____

Date ____ / ____ / ____

Height / Weight _____ / _____

AND I GREW

AND I GREW

AND I GREW

Things that are Special about _____
                    (To be written by parent or other family member)

25 I AM . . .

This highly interactive activity helps students identify the main contributors to their self-esteem as well as giving them the chance to affirm each
other with positive feedback.

GOALS

Identify the main characteristics of the individual's Self.

Give positive affirmations to group members.

TIME FRAME

45–50 minutes

AGE GROUP

Adaptable for any

MATERIALS NEEDED

I Am . . . worksheet for each student.

PROCESS

1) Begin with a brief discussion using the following points:

   ● There are many things that go into making up our self-esteem.

   ● Self-esteem involves how we see ourselves as well as the messages
     other people give us about who we are.

   ● For a healthy self-esteem, it is important that we can identify our-
     selves in many ways. For example, if an athlete is only identified by
     his athletic prowess, what happens to his self-esteem if he is injured?
     He doesn't have anything to fall back on—he has nothing else to
     identify himself with.

   ● As you are growing up, it is important that you try many different
     roles and activities to give yourself the benefit of enlarging your self-
     esteem identifiers.

   ● Even now you may have more identifiers than you realize.

   ● How other people feel about us also contributes to our self-esteem.
     Self-esteem has its roots in the way we were treated by our parents

and important others during our early years, and the way family and friends relate to us now is still a big factor in how we feel about ourselves.

● It is important that we help each other by giving as much positive regard to each other as possible.

● We don't have to be best friends with everyone we know, but we can all strive to see the good in each other.

2) Distribute **I Am** Worksheet to each student.

☞ *You may want younger students to color in identifying facial features to create a self portrait. Caution them not to color in the middle part of the body.*

3) Instruct students to write their name across the top of the sheet.

4) On the middle of the body, encourage them to write as many words as possible that identify who they are, for example:

daughter	**student**	**cheerleader**
good speller	**soccer player**	**choir member**
brother	**nephew**	**musician** etc.

5) Encourage them to include as many identifiers as possible.

6) When completed, tell the students that they are now going to have the chance to give **POSITIVE** feedback to their fellow students.

7) Use the following instructions for this part of the activity.

➤ Student papers will be passed to you during the next part of this activity.

➤ You are to write positive statements about that person in the space surrounding the body outline. No negative comments allowed!

☞ *Encourage students to think of the things they like and admire about other students in the class, having not only to do with physical appearance, but with the strengths and talents they notice in that other person. Encourage them to try to write something different about each person.*

➤ If you really cannot say anything positive about this person, do not write anything.

☞ *The word "nice" cannot be used. It's a cop-out word used when we can't think of anything else to say.*

➤ The purpose of this part of the activity is to help each other know that there are special things about him or her that we recognize and appreciate. Negative comments hurt.

8) Begin this section of the activity by having students hand their sheet to the person directly behind them.

9) When students have finished writing something **POSITIVE** on the sheet, they are to call out the name of the person whose sheet they have so that another student can take the sheet and write on it.

   ☞ *This gets a little noisy but is an energizing part of the activity as students hear their names called out and sheets are exchanged.*

10) When all writing is completed, collect the sheets and make comments on some of the things students have written.

   ☞ *This will also give you a chance to spot any negatives that may have been written. If there are any, cross them out with a magic marker and mention how hurtful negative comments can be.*

11) Return the sheets to the students. Give them a few moments to look over their sheets and then use the following points for a discussion:

   ✔ How does it feel to have positive comments written about you?

   ✔ How did it feel to write good things about other students?

   ✔ How difficult was it to come up with something different about each student?

   ✔ Based on some of the comments that have been read and shared, what do you think is the basic level of appreciation in this class? Is it superficial, or does it show that we really try and see the special things in each other?

I AM

26 WHO AM I?

This activity helps students identify twenty of their lifestyle characteristics and helps them examine those that contribute to or detract from their personal wellness.

GOALS

Identify personal lifestyle characteristics.

Identify those things that we would like to change, why we would like to change them and how we can go about making the changes.

Identify those characteristics that, continued into the future, could become risk factors for health and well-being.

Identify those characteristics that, continued into the future, will strengthen health and well-being.

Identify those characteristics that are supported by peer group, and those that are important as personal values.

TIME FRAME

1–2 class periods

AGE GROUP

Junior and senior high

MATERIALS NEEDED

Who Am I? worksheet for each student.

PROCESS

1) Use the following points for an opening discussion:

- All of us have things about ourselves that we would like to change.

- Some of us have characteristics that, continued over a lifetime, could lead to health risks, disability or even death.

- We also have characteristics that, continued over a lifetime, will contribute to our health and well-being.

- Sometimes our lifestyle habits are influenced by our friends and it is important to know which of our lifestyle choices are ours and which have been influenced by our peers.

- It is important to identify both positive and negative lifestyle characteristics as early as possible, so that we can change what needs to be changed before it becomes a problem, and we can celebrate and strengthen the positive things we do for ourselves to provide the greatest opportunity for extended health and well-being.

- You are a mixture of all your individual characteristics—both strengths and weaknesses.

- This activity will help you identify the lifestyle characteristics that make up your life—both positive and negative—and the effect that these characteristics can have on your life now and in the future, as well as which of your habits/behaviors are based on personal values and which are as a result of the influence of your friends.

2) Distribute a **Who Am I?** worksheet to each student.

3) Write the following wellness areas on the board:
   P – Physical: nutrition/fitness/smoking/drugs/alcohol
   M – Mental: attitude/self-esteem
   E – Emotional: ability to handle feelings
   S – Spiritual: sense and purpose of meaning; faith
   I – Intellectual: motivation and drive to learn/pride in ability to learn

4) Use the following instructions for completing the worksheet:

   ➤ Do not write your name on these worksheets.

   ➤ Write 20 short phrases that describe your lifestyle habits. These may include characteristics such as swimmer, smoker, runner, chocolate lover, alcohol consumer, computer nut, bookworm, or any others that describe your current lifestyle habits.

   ➤ Put a "P" next to those descriptors that make you proud.

   ➤ Put a "C" next to those you would like to change.

   ➤ Briefly describe why you would want to change this characteristic.

   ➤ Put an "R" next to any descriptors that could turn into risk factors, i.e., smoking, alcohol/drug consumption, etc.

   ➤ Put a "W" next to any of your descriptors that, over a lifetime, could contribute to your health and well-being.

©1994 Whole Person Press 210 W Michigan Duluth MN 55802   (800) 247-6789

➤ Put an "F" next to those characteristics that are shared by most of your friends.

➤ Put a "V" next to those things that are important personal values to you.

➤ Looking at the list of wellness areas on the board, use the code to identify the areas of wellness which are represented by each of your lifestyle characteristics.

5) You can do one of two things with the activity at this point depending on how comfortable your students are in discussing personal things within the group setting:

Plan 1   Collect all sheets and compile a composite of the answers given for discussion during the next class:

Make notes on the following items:

   a. Characteristics that students considered risk factors.
   b. The characteristics they would most like to change.
   c. The characteristics of which they are most proud.
   d. Characteristics students considered to be wellness enhancing.
   e. The number of characteristics that fell into various wellness areas.
   f. The kinds of personal values that were indicated.
   g. The characteristics that were shared by peers.

Plan 2   Have students share from their own lists in small groups and/ or as a large group.

☞ *Plan 1 is better because it provides the opportunity to see how all students are feeling without having to share personally, but if time is limited, Plan 2 can be good for discussion.*

6) Use the following questions for discussion:

✔ Are there any generalities we can see about the kinds of qualities listed by this class?

✔ Did characteristics fall into any predominate areas of wellness, or were we fairly balanced?

✔ What were the major risk factors identified by this class?

✔ What were the major wellness-enhancing characteristics identified by the class?

✔ What kinds of changes were most noted? What areas of wellness did they come from?

✔ What kinds of personal values are important to this group?

✔ Which characteristics are most supported by the peer group?

✔ How do we go about making changes in things that we see as needing change?

✔ Will any of these things change automatically as you get older?

✔ Will peer influence change? How will this affect your lifestyle characteristics?

TRAINER'S NOTES

©1994 Whole Person Press 210 W Michigan Duluth MN 55802   (800) 247-6789

WHO AM I? WORKSHEET

List 20 lifestyle habits/characteristics that describe you:

1.

2.

3.

4.

5.

6.

7.

8.

9.

10.

11.

12.

13.

14.

15.

16.

17.

18.

19.

20.

PERSONAL WELLNESS

27 WELLNESS RATING (p 82)

Students use a continuum to help them assess their personal levels of wellness. (At the start of your wellness program and then periodically throughout it.)

28 WHERE DO WE GO FROM HERE? (p 89)

Self-responsibility is at the heart of wellness. This activity helps students see how their various life roles offer them opportunities to make a difference in their own health and well-being and that of others. (30–45 minutes)

29 THE MAGIC WISH (p 92)

This guided imagery exercise helps students focus on what they would wish for to make their lives the best they can be. (15–30 minutes)

30 WHAT DO I HAVE GOING FOR ME? (p 95)

This activity helps students evaluate their strengths as they look toward building a wellness lifestyle.(10–30 minutes)

27 WELLNESS RATING

Students use a continuum to help them assess their personal levels of wellness.

GOALS

Encourage students to analyze their personal wellness levels.

Encourages the class to look at the group's "wellness average" and discuss changes that might be expected as a result of a wellness program.

Help students become aware of areas in their lives which could benefit by some wellness goal setting.

TIME FRAME

At the start of your wellness program and then periodically throughout it.

AGE GROUP

Junior and senior high

MATERIALS NEEDED

Wellness Continuum and Class Average Chart (Plan A); **My Present Wellness Level** worksheets (Plan B).

PROCESS

☞ *There are several ways to proceed with this activity. How you proceed will depend on what you want your class to accomplish.*

The primary objective is to gather a class "average" of each individual's self-assessed position on the wellness continuum at the beginning of your wellness program, perhaps in the middle and at the end of the program.

By using the results of this activity you can plan other activities to help students identify areas in which they may want to do some personal assessment and goal setting.

PLAN A

☞ Before starting Plan A, you will want to copy the Wellness Continuum, below, on the chalkboard.

1	2	3	4	5	6	7	8	9	10

Low level	*OK/Fine*	*High Level*
Worseness	*Not Sick*	*Wellness*

1) After introducing the topic of wellness, illustrate the process of "getting well" by using the wellness continuum, which you have copied on the board.

2) Explain the continuum by making the following points:

- Number 5 on the continuum represents "fine." I'm not sick. I'm just OK. This is the point where the medical model brings us when we get "well" after being ill.

- From 5 to 1 on the continuum is the area of "Low Level Wellness." This is the area that represents:

  (4) not feeling good;

  (3) feeling worse;

  (2) sick;

  (1) very ill/dead.

- This can represent physical or mental/emotional well-being. Individual interpretation is important here, particularly with young people whose mental/emotional levels of wellness or worseness may be more critical than their physical levels.

- From 5 to 10 on the continuum is the area of "High Level Wellness." This is the area that represents:

  (6) feeling pretty good/aware of myself and my life;

  (7) feeling even better/excited about life and its possibilities;

  (8) feeling even better/actively participating in making my life better;

  (9) I'm just getting better and better! I'm having a ball in my life; liking myself and others; recognizing and working toward my potential and enjoying the journey;

  (10) I'm the BEST I CAN EVER BE.

3) After explaining the continuum, discuss the following points:

- We are all different.

- We are all at different levels on the continuum, based on our lifestyles and attitudes.

- We are all in the process of "becoming."

    ✔ Are any of us ever the best we can be?

4) Have students assess where they are on the continuum. This is a private process and doesn't have to be shared with the rest of the class. Have students record the number that best represents where they see themselves on the wellness continuum. Have them record their number in a place where they can keep it for future reference and record it on a slip of paper which they will pass to you.

5) After receiving all of the results, add them and figure the class "wellness average." Discuss the finding with the class noting any unusual findings like numbers on either extreme of the continuum.

    ☞ *If you have any results at the far left end of the continuum, encourage that student to speak to you in private. This could be a cry for help and should not go unheeded. If you have any results at 10, remark that we are all in the process of getting better and better. Are we ever as "well" as we can be? Can we ever truly be a 10? Why or why not? This can generate some lively class discussion!*

6) Repeat this activity several times throughout the program, particularly at the end of the program. How has the class average changed over time? Point out that our levels of wellness are not static; in fact, they can change from day to day—sometimes hour to hour, particularly in the emotional, mental, social, and even physical levels.

7) At the session following the self-assessment, show the students a continuum chart with all the individual self assessments indicated.

8) Use the following questions as discussion points:

    ✔ Look at the various designations along the continuum. Where do most of us seem to place ourselves?

    ✔ Why do you think that is?

9) Close Plan A with the following statement:

- Look at your own record of where you placed yourself on this continuum. A self-rating of 1 means that we should probably call the emergency team for life support for you. A self-rating of 10 means that we probably aren't going to be able to stand you for the rest of the day and, because you feel so absolutely on top of the world, you're going to drive the rest of us poor mortals crazy!

PLAN B

1) To get a better idea of where your students see themselves, have them complete the above activity, but this time, use an individual continuum for each area of wellness on the worksheet.

2) Next, have students assess where they fall on each continuum, note the numbers for themselves on a continuum sheet they will keep and on one which they will give to you (without name).

3) Have students compute an average for themselves.

4) Discuss as in Plan A.

VARIATION

■ You might want to combine Plan A and Plan B.

Have students assess where they are on the overall wellness continuum as in Plan A.

During the next session, have them compute their average based on individual areas as in Plan B.

Have them compare their scores for the two. What did the comparison show? Are they about the same? Very different? Slightly different? Why? Are they stronger in one area than they thought they might be?

■ Complete this activity for just self-esteem.

The continuum, numbered from 1–10, would have similar designations to the wellness continuum:

1) I really hate myself;

2) I can't stand myself;

3) I have some real problems, and generally, I don't care very much for myself;

4) I'm not really crazy about myself, but I don't hate myself;

5) I'm OK;

6) I'm better than OK;

7) I may have some faults, but generally, I like myself;

8) I'm getting better by the day;

9) I really think I'm an OK person; I really like myself.

10) I'm my own best friend; I'm GOOD STUFF!

Have class members locate themselves on the continuum, note their levels for themselves, and pass in their assessment to you on an unsigned piece of paper.

Compute the class "average" and use this average as a discussion starter for ways in which teens can help themselves and others increase their levels of self-esteem.

Repeat throughout the year and particularly at the end of your self-esteem program.

MY PRESENT WELLNESS LEVEL

Circle the number on each continuum that best describes your current status for that category.

I. PHYSICAL

| 1 | 2 | 3 | 4 | 5 | 6 | 7 | 8 | 9 | 10 |

Totally Unfit   *Totally Fit*

II. EMOTIONAL

| 1 | 2 | 3 | 4 | 5 | 6 | 7 | 8 | 9 | 10 |

An Emotional   *Feeling*
Wreck   *Great!*

III. INTELLECTUAL

| 1 | 2 | 3 | 4 | 5 | 6 | 7 | 8 | 9 | 10 |

Brain Dead   *Fit To*
                                                                    Learn

IV. SPIRITUAL

| 1 | 2 | 3 | 4 | 5 | 6 | 7 | 8 | 9 | 10 |

No Peace   *Peace And*
                                                                    Serenity

V. RELATIONSHIPS

| 1 | 2 | 3 | 4 | 5 | 6 | 7 | 8 | 9 | 10 |

Alone And   *Getting*
Lonely   *Along Well*

VI. LIFE WORK

| 1 | 2 | 3 | 4 | 5 | 6 | 7 | 8 | 9 | 10 |

No Goals   *Really Looking*
                                                                    Forward To Life

VII. NUTRITION

1	2	3	4	5	6	7	8	9	10

A Nutritional
Wreck

I Eat Well And
FEEL GREAT!

VIII. ENERGY LEVELS

1	2	3	4	5	6	7	8	9	10

Can't Get Out
Of My Own Way

Energy To
Spare

IX. STRESS

1	2	3	4	5	6	7	8	9	10

Stressed To
The Max

In Control

X. OVERALL HEALTH

1	2	3	4	5	6	7	8	9	10

Dead

ALIVE!

XI. DRUGS/ALCOHOL/SMOKING

1	2	3	4	5	6	7	8	9	10

Abuser

DRUG FREE!

XII. ENVIRONMENTAL

1	2	3	4	5	6	7	8	9	10

Wasteful

Preserver

TOTALS

To calculate your present wellness level, add up the numbers you have circled on each continuum, then divide by 12.

Total _____ ÷12 = _____ (Your Wellness Level)

28 WHERE DO WE GO FROM HERE?

Self-responsibility is at the heart of wellness. This activity helps students see how their various life roles offer them opportunities to make a difference in their own health and well-being and that of others.

GOALS

Identify various roles that students will assume during their lives.

Assess how, in these various roles, individuals can affect their own well-being as well as that of others.

Look at issues of self-responsibility and ways to increase the level of self-responsibility in teens.

TIME FRAME

30–45 minutes

AGE GROUP

Junior and senior high

MATERIALS NEEDED

Role Assessment worksheet for each student.

PROCESS

1) Introduce the activity with the following discussion points:

   ● More and more individuals are recognizing the importance of their role in their own health care and wellness.

   ● Individuals are taking more responsibility for their wellness.

   ● More and more people are also involved in promoting wellness for other people.

   ● In our lives, each of us will take on many roles and responsibilities.

2) Make a list on the chalkboard of the various roles that students can look forward to assuming during their lifetime. These can include, but are not limited to, the following:

Professional

Family Member

Parent

Consumer

Employer

Employee

Citizen

3) Instruct students to list on their worksheets the six roles they think will be of the most importance to them during their lives.

4) Have them think about the health promoting actions they could take in each of these roles and list them on their sheets.

5) After students have completed their individual worksheets, discuss each of the roles listed on the board as to the kinds of health promoting activities that could be part of each of these roles.

6) Use the following points for discussion:

✔ Which of these roles do you already assume?

✔ In the roles you already assume, what kinds of things can you do NOW to promote health and well-being in yourself and for others?

✔ For the roles you have yet to assume, how can you prepare as a young person to take on the challenges of each of these roles in the area of health and wellness?

✔ Do you think self-responsibility is something that teens give much thought to?

✔ What steps could we take to increase the level of interest in self-responsibility in teens?

ROLE ASSESSMENT WORKSHEET

List six of the most important roles you feel you will assume during your life. Under each, write a few of the things you feel you can do to promote health and wellness in yourself and in others.

1.

2.

3.

4.

5.

6.

29 THE MAGIC WISH

This guided imagery exercise helps students focus on what they would wish for to make their lives the best they can be.

GOALS

Experience the effects of visual imagery.

Help students focus on their goals for personal well-being for the future.

Encourage class sharing and communication.

TIME FRAME

15–30 minutes

AGE GROUP

Particularly effective for younger elementary, but can be adapted for most age groups

MATERIALS NEEDED

Brown lunch bag for each student.

PROCESS

1) Instruct students to take the brown lunch bag with them and find a comfortable position on the floor.

2) Give the following instructions for the imagery exercise:

➤ Lie on the floor in a comfortable position making sure you are not touching the person next to you.

➤ Keep your eyes closed throughout the activity.

➤ Don't talk.

➤ Hold your bags quietly during the activity until I tell you what to do with them.

➤ Now, close your eyes. Get comfortable. For today, we are going to take a special journey to visit a very special person.

➤ But before we go, we need to be very relaxed. So, as I count to 4, I want you to take a long, slow, deep breath. Ready, In . . . 1 . . . 2 . . . 3 . . . 4 . . . Now, as I say "out" and count to 4, I want you to let go of that breath. Ready, Out . . . 1 . . . 2 . . . 3 . . . 4. In . . .1 . . . 2 . . . 3 . . . 4. Out . . . 1 . . . 2 . . . 3 . . . 4. Ready, In . . .1 . . . 2 . . . 3 . . . 4.

3) Read the **Wizard** script on page 94.

4) After reading the script, have the students come quietly and sit in a circle around you, holding their bags tightly closed.

5) Ask the children to tell you about what they saw on their journey.

✔ What colors were the flowers?

✔ What colors were the birds?

✔ What kinds of trees were there in the forest?

✔ How did you feel as you walked along in the forest?

✔ Were you afraid?

✔ What did the Wizard look like?

6) Now have one child at a time open his bag and share his magic wish.

7) Comment positively on each child's wish for the future.

8) Ask each child how he or she will come to have this magic wish, for example:

Child: My magic wish is to have lots of friends.
Instructor: How will you get your wish?
Child: By being a friend myself.

Child: My magic wish is to have a strong body.
Instructor: How will you get your wish?
Child: By exercising and eating right every day.

☞ *You will probably have at least one child say that his wish is to have lots of money. That's okay. Ask the child, "How will you get it?" (By working hard. When you study hard in school, you will be really smart so you will be able to find a good job so you can have money, if that is what is important to you.)*

9) Use the following points for discussion about ways they can make their wishes come true.

✔ Who is responsible for making your wish come true?

➤ Who really is the Wizard? You Are! You are the magic person who can make all the wishes for the future come true.

THE WIZARD Script

Now that you're feeling calm and relaxed I want you to go on a trip through a beautiful forest with me.

Can you see the trees and flowers? They're everywhere. Look at all the colors. There are lots of beautiful birds, too, and there is a gentle breeze blowing that cools us as we walk along. Let the sunshine warm you. It's a perfect day, and you feel really happy as we all walk along.

Now, we're coming around a bend in the path and right in front of us is the house of the Wizard. The Wizard is a wonderful, old, old, old, kind and loving magician. He has the power to make wishes for the future come true, and he has invited all of us to his house today to see what our magic wishes are for the future.

See yourself sitting in a circle around the Wizard, listening to his soft, gentle voice talking to you about his forest, his birds and his trees.

Notice how safe and warm you feel. The Wizard is asking each person what his or her magic wish is for the future. "What would you like to have in the future that would make your life healthy and happy? Would you wish for good health? or a happy family? or lots of friends? What would your wish be?" asks the Wizard.

As you tell the Wizard your wish quietly in your mind, the Wizard touches you on your forehead with his magic wand and places your wish inside the bag you have brought with you.

The Wizard is asking you what you want for your life. What is your magic wish for the future? Quietly open your bag so that the Wizard can put your wish inside. Once it is inside, close the top of the bag tightly so that your wish can't escape. Now, we are leaving the Wizard. Quietly say good-bye and wave as we walk back down the path back through the forest, back to our classroom.

Now, very quietly and slowly open your eyes, stretch and sit up where you are.

30 WHAT DO I HAVE GOING FOR ME?

This activity helps students evaluate their strengths as they look toward building a wellness lifestyle.

GOALS

Evaluate personal strengths.

Celebrate who we already are.

TIME FRAME

10–30 minutes

AGE GROUP

Upper elementary through senior high

MATERIALS NEEDED

What I Have Going For Me worksheet for each student.

PROCESS

1) Distribute **What I Have Going for Me** worksheets.

2) Begin with the following discussion:

   ● Wellness isn't just a bunch of do's and don'ts. Rather, it is a choice we make to live our lives the best we can, building on our strengths and working on our limitations to live the best life we can.

   ● Part of preparing for this journey is to take stock of what we already do well—what we have going for us in our lives—so that we can celebrate who we are rather than always finding fault with who we are not.

3) Have students complete the **What I Have Going For Me** worksheet.

   ● This activity will help you assess your current and ideal levels of wellness and will help you see what your strengths and weaknesses are.

4) Use the results as a starting point for classroom discussion concerning how wellness begins in our lives.

   ✔ Who helps you get started in your wellness life journey?

✔ What is your biggest strength?

✔ What is your weakest point? How can you strengthen weak points?

✔ What are you most proud of in your wellness journey?

✔ Is wellness important to you? If not, when do you think it will begin to be important to you?

TRAINER'S NOTES

WHAT I HAVE GOING FOR ME, Part 1

For each wellness area, mark on the Present continuum where you see yourself today. On the Future continuum mark where you would like to be in the future: 0 represents "OK", -5 represents dead and buried; +5 represents perfection—whatever that is!

1. PHYSICAL

PRESENT *(where I see myself now)*   FUTURE *(my ideal)*
-5 -4 -3 - 2 -1 0 +1 +2 +3 +4 +5   -5 -4 -3 - 2 -1 0 +1 +2 +3 +4 +5

What do I have going for me? (strength/heredity/energy/exercise program/nutrition)

2. INTELLECTUAL

PRESENT *(where I see myself now)*   FUTURE *(my ideal)*
-5 -4 -3 - 2 -1 0 +1 +2 +3 +4 +5   -5 -4 -3 - 2 -1 0 +1 +2 +3 +4 +5

What do I have going for me? (humor/insight/memory/creativity/ curiosity/motivation)

3. SPIRITUAL

PRESENT *(where I see myself now)*   FUTURE *(my ideal)*
-5 -4 -3 - 2 -1 0 +1 +2 +3 +4 +5   -5 -4 -3 - 2 -1 0 +1 +2 +3 +4 +5

What do I have going for me? (worship life/strong values/firm beliefs)

4. EMOTIONAL

PRESENT *(where I see myself now)*   FUTURE *(my ideal)*
-5 -4 -3 - 2 -1 0 +1 +2 +3 +4 +5   -5 -4 -3 - 2 -1 0 +1 +2 +3 +4 +5

What do I have going for me? (self-confidence/ability to express feelings/comfortable with myself and others)

5. SOCIAL

PRESENT *(where I see myself now)*   FUTURE *(my ideal)*
-5 -4 -3 - 2 -1 0 +1 +2 +3 +4 +5   -5 -4 -3 - 2 -1 0 +1 +2 +3 +4 +5

What do I have going for me? (friends/family/clubs/ability to play/get along well with others)

6. LIFESTYLE

PRESENT *(where I see myself now)*   FUTURE *(my ideal)*
-5 -4 -3 - 2 -1 0 +1 +2 +3 +4 +5   -5 -4 -3 - 2 -1 0 +1 +2 +3 +4 +5

What do I have going for me? (hobbies/good habits/ways of relaxing/avoiding chemicals/ healthy habits)

WHAT I HAVE GOING FOR ME, Part 2

ASSESSMENT

Now list your strengths for each area as you see them. After looking at each area of wellness, analyze the areas that need growth and change for you to reach your desired level as well as the things you can start doing to improve your level of wellness in those areas.

In which areas am I strongest?

In which areas do I need growth and change in order to reach my desired future levels?

Things I can start doing to improve my level of wellness in each area:

What I Need to Do   **When I Need to Do This**

1.

2.

3.

4.

5.

VALUES

31 RECOGNIZING OUR VALUES

Students examine the values-formation process and apply it to typical situations facing many teens.

GOALS

Examining the values-formation process.

Examine the impact of peer influence on values formation in teens.

Recognize that we are the ultimate voice in our own values formation.

TIME FRAME

45–50 minutes

AGE GROUP

Junior and senior high

MATERIALS NEEDED

Values chart (see *Step 2*) Scenarios for each group of 3–4 students.

PROCESS

1) Begin with an introductory discussion:

- No one can make us do anything. "They" don't control our lives.

- Part of becoming a self-responsible person is recognizing how much we give in to others' opinions, what the consequences are to our own value structure, and what our alternatives are in these situations.

- Sometimes we lose sight of our own values as we try to fit in with the peer group.

- It's difficult to stick with our values when we are in the process of defining who we are as well as what is important to us in our lives and at the same time fit in with the group.

- What is a value? Values provide the basis for our decision-making process. We use our values to make decisions about our lives and our lifestyles and our behaviors.

- All of us, even adults, are at times confused about our values—which ones to hang on to, which ones to let go of, which ones to change. When we are confronted with a conflict in our values, it leaves us feeling uncomfortable and stressed.

- There are times in our lives when we must make decisions and choices about our health and habits. It is a good idea to think about how we will handle these situations before we are involved in the emotions of the moment.

- This is not the same as **worrying** about what will happen, but it involves **planning** strategies about how we will handle these situations when they arise.

- Adolescent values are very difficult because part of growing up is deciding which values you are going to carry over from your childhood when you accepted everything, and which values you are going to let go of and replace with other values.

- Teens often "try on" values for size, until they find one that "fits." The "fit" is often a result of the standing in the peer group.

- There are certain steps we go through to establish a value. These steps will help us decide what we would be willing to stand up for— what things we have determined to be important for our lives that we are willing to defend.

2) Summarize the following **Values Processes** on newsprint and display.

Choosing Freely: No one makes the choice for you; no one influences your decisions. You choose because it is right for you, not because you are coerced by others' opinions.

Consequences: Choosing after consideration of what could happen as a result of your decision. What might happen if you choose this behavior or support this value? Will it have positive or negative effects on your life and health?

Alternatives: Choosing after considering your options. What could you do instead of this? Would it be better or worse? Who would it benefit? What would the reaction be from others around you?

Prizing one's beliefs and behaviors: Are you proud of your decision? Could/would you tell the world about your decision, or are there some people—like your parents or younger brothers and sisters—whom you would rather not have know about your decision? Why?

©1994 Whole Person Press 210 W Michigan Duluth MN 55802   (800) 247-6789

Acting on one's belief: Have you acted on your decision? Have you acted on it with **repition** and **consistency**, or do you keep changing your mind?

3) Divide the class into groups of 3–4.

4) Make sure the **values processes** are displayed in front of the room.

5) Give each group one of the values problems listed on page 103 (or one of your own).

6) Have groups decide on the most important value in their situation, then list a series of alternatives and consequences for each situation—at least one bad one and one good one for each situation.

7) Instruct them to decide if the alternatives would have been chosen freely by the individual or if he or she would have been coerced by the force of the peer group.

8) After listing the alternatives, have students rank them from most acceptable to least acceptable.

9) Finally, the students should decide if they would actually **act on** the list of alternatives. Would they actually consider using any of the alternatives, or did they just come up with the list to satisfy the activity?

10) Gather the group together and ask for observations and reports on their group process.

11) As each group reports, ask the following questions:

   ✔ What affect did the peer group ultimately have on the individual?

   ✔ What affect did the individuals within the group have on the group's decision concerning alternatives?

   ✔ Do you think you can generalize your results across the teen experience? Do you think most teens would have chosen the way your group did? Why or why not?

   ✔ Do you think most teens think for themselves, or are they ultimately influenced by the will of the group?

   ✔ What happens when a person goes against the will of the group?

VALUES PROCESS scenarios

1) Everyone in the group smokes but John. Although no one has said anything, he feels pressured to either join in or not be accepted by the group.

2) Jill has been dating Bob for six months. He is beginning to put pressure on her to have sex. She made herself a promise to wait until marriage, but Bob says that since they are so close, sex would be okay, and besides, if she really loves him. . . .

3) All the kids are going to a party where alcohol will be served. Jim has been invited to the party, but he has never approved of drinking.

4) Toni's parents are out of town for the weekend. The most popular kid in school—the one Toni most wants to be friends with—has found out and suggested that the gang get together at Toni's house for a party.

5) Todd has been having trouble in chemistry. He has the chance to get the answers to the test for tomorrow from a former student. Todd feels pretty confident about doing well on this test, but if he had the answers. . . .

The values process used here is based on the work of Simon and Kirchenbaum.

32 MAYBE I WILL, MAYBE I WON'T

This activity focuses on some of the "shoulds" that students have been given about their lives and health and helps them clarify which ones they have freely adopted for themselves.

GOALS

Examine the "should" messages that have been given to us by parents and others about our health.

Discover which "shoulds" we have changed into personal choices.

Clarify self-care values.

TIME FRAME

20–30 minutes

AGE GROUP

Middle elementary through senior high

MATERIALS NEEDED

The "Shoulds" In My Life worksheet for each student.

PROCESS

1) Begin with the following discussion:

   ● Sometimes it seems like people are always telling us what to do—how to take care of ourselves, and what will happen to us if we don't. It gets a little overwhelming sometimes.

   ● If we listened to everyone, we would probably be a little crazy, trying to please all those people.

   ✔ What have you been told in your life that you "should" do to take care of yourself?

   ✔ Who gave you most of your "shoulds" when you were little? Now?

2) Distribute a worksheet to each student.

3) On the worksheet, have students list their five biggest "shoulds" in each category—parents, teachers, and friends.

4) Next to each of the "shoulds," have students mark which ones they participate in willingly by putting a "W" next to them, which they do only when they absolutely have to by putting a "D" (don't like them) next to those items, and an "R" next to those things they absolutely refuse to do.

5) Have them look over their sheets and reflect on the following questions:

✔ Who do you listen to most willingly?

✔ Why don't you do all the "shoulds" people tell you to do?

✔ Are there any "shoulds" that you don't like to do that you know you probably ought to do?

✔ The "shoulds" that you **refuse** to do: Why do you **refuse** to do them? (Probably because you don't **want** to)

✔ The "shoulds" that you **do** do: Why do you do them? (Because you **choose** to do them . . . because you see their importance in your life.)

6) Have students mark the "shoulds" that they have willingly changed to "I choose to" with an asterix (*).

7) Use the following points for discussion:

✔ How does just changing the words from "should" to "I choose to" change the feeling you have about the "shoulds" you have marked?

✔ Why have you willingly changed some of your "shoulds" to "I choose to"?

✔ Can you see why you may refuse to do some of the "shoulds" people give you because you cannot freely choose them for yourself?

✔ Which "shoulds" that you are rejecting today may be on your willing list 5 years from now? 10 years from now? Never?

✔ What will get you to change your "shoulds" to "I choose to"?

✔ Which section had most of your accepted "shoulds"?

✔ Which section had most of your rejected "shoulds"?

✔ Would your list have been any different when you were five years old? Why? How?

✔ How many of your refusals are because you are an adolescent and are feeling rebellious?

✔ Do you think this will change?

✔ Are teens more likely to accept "shoulds" from their friends than from their families?

✔ Do you ever experience any inner conflict when the "shoulds" from your friends clash with the "shoulds" from your parents?

8) Point out that "shoulding" (irrational thinking) leads to worry, stress, low self-esteem, and low productivity.

➤ Ask students to talk about any of their "shoulds" that are causing them to worry, feel guilty, or feel bad about themselves.

➤ Point out that it is normal for all of us to—at some point during our lives—rebel against the "shoulds" that other people give us.

➤ Explain that it is a normal part of growing up to examine the values that others have given us to make sure they are personal choices.

9) Ask students to discuss how they can clarify their values so that they know what their true, freely chosen values are and to be sure that they are not just following in the path of other people.

THE "SHOULDS" IN MY LIFE

The five biggest "shoulds" my parents have told me are:

1.

2.

3.

4.

5.

The five biggest "shoulds" my friends have told me are:

1.

2.

3.

4.

5.

The five biggest "shoulds" my teachers have told me are:

1.

2.

3.

4.

5.

Which "shoulds" do you do willingly?
Mark with a "W."

Which "shoulds" do you do only when you absolutely have to?
Mark with a "D."

Which "shoulds" do you absolutely refuse to do?
Mark with an "R."

©1994 Whole Person Press 210 W Michigan Duluth MN 55802   (800) 247-6789

33 I SAID NO!

This short exercise helps students examine the use of saying "no" in their lives.

GOALS

Look at our ability to say "no" in our lives.

Observe how we have used "no" in our lives.

Examine how we can strengthen our ability to use "no" to our best advantage.

Realize that "no" can have a negative effect on our lives if it keeps us from taking advantage of good opportunities.

TIME FRAME

15–20 minutes

AGE GROUP

Upper elementary through senior high

MATERIALS NEEDED

No Inventory worksheet for each student.

PROCESS

1) Begin by asking the following questions:

   ✔ Who do you have the easiest time saying no to?

   ✔ Who do you have the most difficult time saying no to?

2) Have a discussing using the following points:

   ● Saying "no" is sometimes difficult because it puts us up against the people we care most about: our friends.

   ● Teen years are a time of breaking away from many of the things our parents have told us. It is a time of striking out on our own to discover our own values.

   ● Sometimes we make mistakes. This is normal. Mistakes aren't the end of the world no matter how serious. They happen. They say you are growing and changing. Even serious mistakes can be the beginning of a growth process.

● We all experience times when we look back over our lives and wish we had done some things differently.

● We also have times when we have been proud of ourselves for making the decisions we made and sticking by them.

● And sometimes we have let opportunities get by us because we **did** say no and wish we had had the courage to say yes.

● It's time to check the condition of your **no** inventory.

3) Distribute the **No Inventory** worksheets to each student.

4) Have them spend a few minutes completing the inventory.

5) As a group, share some of the responses individuals are comfortable with.

6) Ask the following questions:

✔ Which of your categories had the most items?

✔ What does this tell you about yourself?

✔ Have you missed any opportunities in your life because you didn't have the courage to say "yes" instead of "no"?

✔ Have you had times in your life when you have been proud of yourself for being able to say no?

✔ Have you ever been disappointed in yourself for not being able to say no?

✔ Does your ability to say no have anything to do with your dependence on your peer group?

✔ How has your ability to say no to your parents changed over the years?

✔ What are some things we could do to strengthen our ability to say no when we need to?

✔ What is the biggest difficulty in saying no?

MY "NO" INVENTORY

Times I should have said "no" and didn't:

Times I said "no" and was glad I did:

Times I said "no" and wish I hadn't:

34 CULTURAL WELLNESS VALUES

This activity helps students identify wellness values that are present in their culture.

GOALS

Examine the presence or absence of wellness values in the surrounding culture.

Observe the presence of balance or imbalance in the kinds and amounts of wellness values in various parts of the culture.

Examine ways we can increase the wellness value of our surrounding environment.

TIME FRAME

15–20 minutes

AGE GROUP

Adaptable for any age group

MATERIALS NEEDED

Wellness Values worksheet for each student.

PROCESS

1) Begin the activity with the following discussion:

- For wellness to become an accepted philosophy it needs to be an accepted part of our societal values about our personal well-being.

  ✔ Does wellness exist outside this classroom? Do you ever hear the word anywhere else?

  ✔ Do you see any evidence of wellness lifestyles and values in your environment and culture?

- Let's spend a few minutes examining our culture and see if we can identify any wellness values that may be present.

2) Distribute the **Wellness Values** worksheets to each student.

3) Give the following instructions for completing the worksheet:

➤ Write down any wellness values that you have observed as part of each of the listed categories.

➤ After you have completed each category, use the wellness code on your worksheets to identify which area of wellness is involved in each of the values you have observed.

4) After completion of the worksheet, use the following questions for discussion:

✔ Was it difficult to find wellness values associated with any particular area?

✔ Which of your areas had the most values?

✔ Which had the fewest?

✔ Did any single category contain values from more than one area of wellness?

✔ Which was your most balanced area?

✔ Which was your most unbalanced area, one containing values from only one or two areas of wellness?

✔ Does your culture help or hinder you in your efforts toward building a wellness lifestyle?

✔ What can we do to help improve our wellness culture?

✔ Do you think the idea of wellness will ever be a cultural norm?

WELLNESS VALUES

Briefly note the wellness values you observe in each of the following:

YOUR FAMILY

YOUR FRIENDS

THE NATION

THE CHURCH

SCHOOL

Use the following code to identify the areas of wellness that are associated with each of your identified values:

P – Physical wellness;
E – Emotional wellness;
S – Spiritual wellness;
I – Intellectual wellness;
M – Mental wellness/self-esteem;
E – Environmental wellness.

©1994 Whole Person Press 210 W Michigan Duluth MN 55802   (800) 247-6789

35 LOOKING FROM BOTH SIDES

This activity encourages students to look at both sides of an issue in order to clarify their own personal values regarding substance abuse.

GOALS

Clarify individual values regarding substance abuse.

Practice arguing both sides of a question.

Examine real-life situations through role play.

TIME FRAME

Two class periods

AGE GROUP

All grades

MATERIALS NEEDED

Both Sides theme cards.

PROCESS

1) Divide class into groups of 3–4 students.

2) Distribute a theme card to each group.

3) Instruct the students to develop a skit following these guidelines:

➤ Skits should be 3–4 minutes long.

➤ Skits should illustrate the influence of the group on the individual and the influence of the individual on the group.

4) Give students time to develop and rehearse their skit.

5) Have students perform the skit as rehearsed.

6) Ask students to perform the skit again. Tell them that several times during the performance, you will raise your hand to interrupt the action. The person who has just spoken will then change his or her last lines so that they will reflect the opposite view from the one they just portrayed.

7) Have a brief discussion following each skit using the following points:

✔ What was the influence of the individual on the group?

✔ What was the influence of the group on the individual?

✔ Was it hard to switch positions on a point?

✔ Was it difficult to argue for a point to which you are personally opposed?

✔ How does it help to be able to see both sides of a situation?

Both Sides theme cards

You can use the following samples as theme cards, or use whatever other ideas your wish:

1) Two students have cocaine. They are trying to convince a third to join them.

2) Two of the students are parents who smoke. They are telling their child that they do not want her to smoke.

3) One student has a drinking problem. His or her friends are talking to him or her about it.

4) One student's family disapproves of drinking. The other students come from families where drinking is accepted. All are at a party where drinks are available.

5) One student is a drug dealer who owns really nice clothing and lots of gold jewelry. That student is trying to convince the others that dealing is a great way to make money. All players come from low-income families.

6) One student has finally gotten a date with Mr. or Ms. Wonderful. The date is tonight and this person knows that the person they are dating likes to drink. This person has never had alcohol and up to this point, has not wanted alcohol to be part of his or her life. The other students are trying to help him or her make up his or her mind about what to do while at the party they will be attending that night.

7) It's Saturday Night in Smalltown, USA, and there is nothing to do- except get high. One student is the provider of marijuana for the group. The others are split in their feelings about getting high.

©1994 Whole Person Press 210 W Michigan Duluth MN 55802   (800) 247-6789

TRAINER'S NOTES

VALUES

36 BUILDING TRUST (p 118)

For wellness activities to work in the classroom, students must feel free to express their opinions without fear of ridicule. This activity checks out the level of trust among students. (1 or more class periods)

37 A FRIEND IS AS A FRIEND DOES (p 120)

Students compare what they think a friend should be to the qualities they themselves possess. (2 class periods)

38 A FEW OF MY FAVORITE THINGS (p 123)

Students look at how they have grown and changed over the years in relation to their choices of activities and time spent with friends and family. (30–40 minutes)

39 WHO'S RUNNING YOUR LIFE (p 126)

Students examine the power of peers in their lives as they look at their level of self-responsibility. (45–50 minutes)

40 SECRET BUDDIES (p 129)

Students have the opportunity to do kind things for someone else and have the same done for them. (1 week)

36 BUILDING TRUST

For wellness activities to work in the classroom, students must feel free to express their opinions without fear of ridicule. This activity checks out the level of trust among students.

GOALS

Build trust level among class members.

Lay the foundation for valuing and affirming.

Provide classroom "barometer" of trust for facilitators.

TIME FRAME

One class period or more, if needed.

☞ *Let students lead the way in determining the amount of time needed. With some groups, there is significant interest and participation in this activity, which lets you know that a level of trust already exists among class members. With other groups, this activity may be treated in a rather off-handed way. That's okay, too. It will give you a sense of where your students are in their ability to trust each other.*

AGE GROUP

Upper elementary through junior high

MATERIALS

None.

PROCESS

1) Instruct each student to write down something about herself that she does not think anyone else knows.

2) Have the class share with each other in groups of 4–5 students.

3) Ask group members to decide what kind of information was given by each member of the group:

   ✔ Was it **general information** that could be shared with the public?

   ✔ Was it **special information** that would probably only be shared with a friend?

✔ Was it **private information** that one would probably keep to one's self?

4) Reconvene the entire group. Have the spokesperson for each group relate the group's findings. Make sure that individual people are not discussed, but rather, a general summary of information.

5) On the chalkboard, tally the kind of information that was shared.

6) Review the results with the class:

✔ Which category had the most responses?

✔ Why do you think we generated this particular kind of information in this class?

✔ Was there much personal, private information shared? Why or why not?

✔ What is the level of trust in this class?

✔ What could we do to increase the level of trust within this class?

☞ *Discuss with the class the need for keeping information shared within the class. Sharing private information outside the group can shatter group trust and hurt people.*

VARIATION

If you use this activity early in the year or early in your program, expect general, superficial information to be shared. Trust should build as your program continues.

Therefore, you may want to repeat this activity later in the year or program to monitor trust changes within the group. Don't use it often or it will become boring and invasive.

Questions for discussion when you repeat the exercise:

✔ How has the level of trust in this class changed since the first time we did this exercise? (Compare with a copy of the original tally.)

✔ What have we done that has caused our trust levels to change?

✔ What steps can we take from here to continue/reverse this trend?

✔ Do you feel more or less comfortable sharing about yourself with the group this time? Why?

37 A FRIEND IS AS A FRIEND DOES

Students compare what they think a friend should be to the qualities they themselves possess.

GOALS

Analyze the qualities that are important in a friend.

Compare individually chosen friendship qualities with those characteristics that students see in themselves.

TIME FRAME

Initial questioning takes about 10 minutes. Need time to tally results and create a master list. 45–50 minutes for follow-up class period.

AGE GROUP

Upper elementary through senior high

MATERIALS NEEDED

Sheet of paper for each student; **Self-Evaluative Friendship** worksheet for each student; master list of responses for each student.

PROCESS

1) Ask each student to write down ten completions to the following phrase on a sheet of paper:

   A good friend (is) _____ .

2) Collect responses and print a master list for each student.

3) During follow-up class, distribute master lists and instruct students to prioritize them, selecting the twenty most important characteristics of a friend.

4) Have them write the twenty characteristics in the appropriate column on the worksheet.

5) Instruct students to choose the top three characteristics and mark them 1 (most important), 2 (second most important), and 3 (third most important).

6) Discuss which characteristics were chosen as most important by most students.

7) Now have students evaluate themselves, using the characteristics they have individually chosen as those most important for a friend. Instruct them to mark next to each item whether they *always* display that characteristic, *sometimes* display it, or need to *display it more* in their own lives.

8) Use the following points for discussion:

● Along with other decisions, we make decisions regarding the types of people we want as our friends.

✔ How have your requirements for friends changed since you were in the first or second grade? Why?

✔ Do you think those requirements will change for you throughout your life?

● Our behavior can also influence the friendship choices that others make.

✔ How do your requirements for friends compare to your own personal qualities?

✔ Do you have the qualities you look for in a friend?

©1994 Whole Person Press 210 W Michigan Duluth MN 55802   (800) 247-6789

TO HAVE A FRIEND

My choice for the twenty most important characteristics in a friend are:

Characteristic	Always	Sometimes	Need to Display More
1.			
2.			
3.			
4.			
5.			
6.			
7.			
8.			
9.			
10.			
11.			
12.			
13.			
14.			
15.			
16.			
17.			
18.			
19.			
20.			

Once you have completed your list, mark the three characteristics you think are **MOST** important by labeling them with a **1** (most important), **2** (second most important), or **3** (third most important).

Then, note next to each item whether you *always* display that characteristic, *sometimes* display it, or *need to display more* of it in your own life. Do you have the same characteristics you look for in a friend?

©1994 Whole Person Press 210 W Michigan Duluth MN 55802   (800) 247-6789

38 A FEW OF MY FAVORITE THINGS

Students look at how they have grown and changed over the years in relation to their choices of activities and time spent with friends and family.

GOALS

Examine how lifestyles change as we grow.

Examine the differences in time spent with family and friends as we grow up.

Look at the development of both wellness and risk behaviors.

TIME FRAME

30–45 minutes

AGE GROUP

Junior and senior high

MATERIALS NEEDED

My Favorite Things worksheet for each student.

PROCESS

1) Distribute a worksheet to each student.

2) Give the following instructions for filling out the worksheet:

   ☞ *Pause after each step so that students have enough time to complete the instructions.*

   ➤ List your ten favorite things to do in **List A**, beginning with your most favorite.

   ➤ List your ten favorite things when you were six years old in **List B**.

   ➤ In **Column A**, place a check mark next to things you do only with your family. Go to **List B** and place a check mark next to those things that you did only with your family when you were six.

   ➤ In **Column B**, place a check mark next to the things you do only with your friends. Go to **List B** and place a check mark next to those things that you did only with your friends when you were six.

➤ In **Column C**, place a check mark next to the items that contribute to your health and wellness. Do this for both lists.

➤ In **Column D**, place a check mark next to any activities that involve risks to either your health or safety. Do this for both lists.

➤ At the bottom of each list, tally the number of check marks for each column.

3) After completion of the worksheet, lead a discussion by posing the following questions:

✔ Has the time spent with your family changed since you were six? Why? How?

✔ Has the time spent with your friends changed since you were six? Why? How?

✔ How do you feel about these changes?

✔ Do your favorite things involve more or less risk now than they did when you were six? What kinds?

✔ Are your favorite things more or less wellness oriented than when you were six?

✔ Was it more or less comfortable/safe being six than the age you are now?

✔ Do you think your family/friend ratio will change again? When? How? Why?

MY FAVORITE THINGS

Beginning with your most favorite, list your ten most favorite things to do at this time in your life.

List A - Activity	A	B	C	D
1.				
2.				
3.				
4.				
5.				
6.				
7.				
8.				
9.				
10.				

Tally _____

Now list your ten most favorite things when you were six years old.

List B - Activity	A	B	C	D
1.				
2.				
3.				
4.				
5.				
6.				
7.				
8.				
9.				
10.				

Tally _____

39 WHO'S RUNNING YOUR LIFE?

Students examine the power of peers in their lives as they look at their level of self-responsibility.

GOALS

Evaluate who is most important in our lives.

Discover who impacts the decisions we make.

Reaffirm our ability to make responsible decisions.

TIME FRAME

45–50 minutes

AGE GROUP

Upper elementary through junior high

MATERIALS NEEDED

Who Makes Your Choices? worksheet for each student.

PROCESS

1) Begin with a class discussion using the following points of emphasis:

- Self-responsibility is a central part of a wellness lifestyle.

- To become truly self-responsible, we need to be the ones calling the shots in our lives.

- This is the time in your life when friends are all-important, which is normal. Sometimes, however, you can lose your "self" as you try to fit in with the group.

- It is important to remember that you are a special and unique individual and that you can make decisions for yourself, even if those decisions go against group norms.

- As you try to become more self-responsible, it is important to examine the power of peers and others in your lives and to reaffirm that you CAN make your own decisions based on your personal goals and values.

- As you grow into your teen years, it is normal to want to get away from many of the things that parents and other adults have told you. Friends often determine how you act and what you do with your life.

- However, if you look closely, you will often find that there are many people in your life—some you don't even know personally (like rock stars and public figures)—who influence the way we live, look, and behave.

- Think about who's running your life.

2) Distribute worksheets to students.

3) Give students time to complete the worksheets (about 10 minutes).

4) You can process the activity in several ways:

   a. Discuss as a group.

   b. Discuss in small groups.

   c. Have students hand in sheets without names. Redistribute throughout the class for discussion. This protects the identity of students and may help them be more honest with their answers.

5) Make a classroom tally on the board that summarizes the findings of the class.

6) Use the following questions for discussing results:

   ✔ Who is most important in determining the behavior of this class?

   ✔ Do you think these results would hold true for the entire sixth/seventh/eighth grade population? Why or why not?

   ✔ Do you think most people were honest on this survey? Why or why not?

   ✔ Looking at the results, how has influence changed from the time you were small children? Why?

   ✔ What are the general feelings about how influence will change over the next years?

©1994 Whole Person Press 210 W Michigan Duluth MN 55802   (800) 247-6789

WHO MAKES YOUR CHOICES

Mark each item with the letter that best matches your opinion.

S – Self   **S/B** – Sisters/Brothers
P – Parents   **PG** – Peer Group
BF – Best Friend   **M** – Media Heroes
PF – Public Figures   **O** – Others (specify who)

Who is the most important person who helps you decide . . .

How to dress? _____

How hard to work in school? _____

How to fix your hair? _____

What music to listen to? _____

What to do with your free time? _____

How to spend your money? _____

Whether or not to smoke/drink/try other drugs? _____

What to do with your life? _____

How you feel? _____

Looking at your answers, who seems most important to you?

The following is a list of some of the people in your life. Circle those people who have the most influence on you now.

Put an asterix (*) by those who had the most influence on you when you were six years old.

Put a plus sign (+) by those who you think will have the most influence on you when you are older.

PARENTS

BROTHERS/SISTERS

FAVORITE ROCK STARS, MOVIE STARS, SPORTS FIGURES, ETC.

YOUR BEST FRIEND

YOUR FAVORITE TEACHER

YOUR COACH

YOUR MINISTER

A NEIGHBOR

A RELATIVE

YOUR COUNSELOR

WHO ELSE? _____

40 SECRET BUDDIES

Students have the opportunity to do kind things for someone else and have the same done for them.

GOALS

Provide the opportunity for students to care for each other.

Note what happens in groups when there is a lot of caring going on.

TIME FRAME

One week

AGE GROUP

Any age; particularly effective in junior and senior high

MATERIALS NEEDED

Names of students on small slips of paper; a box; bulletin board space for Secret Buddy exchanges.

PROCESS

1) Write names of students on slips of paper—one name per paper—fold and put into a box.

2) Prepare a bulletin board for Secret Buddy exchange. If possible, have available some of the following items for exchanges: note paper in different colors; markers; thumbtacks; stickers; tape; decorative items (i.e., feathers, pom-pons, glitter, etc.).

3) Have students draw a name.

   ☞ *Allow no trading, moaning or disapproving gestures.*

4) Instruct the class that the name they have drawn is to be their secret buddy for the week.

5) The following are the rules for the Secret Buddy experience:

   ➤ Your job is to make the day better for your buddy without that person knowing it is you. No more than $1 a day can be spent on a buddy, but no money need be spent at all.

   ➤ Use your imagination to create gifts, poetry or special surprises for your buddy.

➤ Do at least one nice thing for your buddy each day.

➤ You can use the Secret Buddy board to deliver your messages/gifts, or you can deliver your message in any way you see fit.

➤ Some ideas for Secret Buddy activities: locker decorations; balloons; message over the P.A. system; poetry; note; snacks, candy or small trinkets; buttons.

➤ Even if this is not your best friend, do one nice thing for this person each day, even if you only leave a "good morning" message on the Buddy Board. It's hurtful to be left out.

6) At the end of the week, each person writes a short piece about his Secret Buddy. Each person reads his piece to the rest of the class, not revealing the name of the Secret Buddy until the very end.

7) A small token of friendship (under $5) may be given to the Secret Buddy at this time.

☞ *It is important for facilitators to keep an eye on the Secret Buddy process, to make sure that all students are receiving some sort of recognition. You may be the Secret Buddy for any student who isn't receiving recognition, or you may ask one of your more caring students if she or he would like to take on an extra Buddy so that no one is left out. This is extremely important.*

8) Use the following points for follow-up discussion:

✔ How did you feel about this activity in the beginning?

✔ How did you feel about it during the week? Was it fun or a burden?

✔ Did you enjoy doing something for someone else? Did you enjoy receiving things for yourself?

✔ Has this activity affected the spirit in class at all?

✔ Did you learn anything about yourself during this process? Did you learn anything about other people during this process?

RESOURCES

WHOLE PERSON ASSOCIATES RESOURCES

Our materials are designed to address the whole person—physical, emotional, mental, spiritual, and social. Developed for trainers by trainers, all of these resources are ready-to-use. Novice trainers will find everything they need to get started, and the expert trainer will discover new ideas and concepts to add to their existing programs.

GROUP PROCESS RESOURCES

All of the exercises in our group process resources encourage interaction between the leader and participants, as well as among the participants. Each exercise includes everything you need to present a meaningful program: goals, optimal group size, time frame, materials list, and the complete process instructions.

WELLNESS ACTIVITIES FOR YOUTH
Volume 1
Sandy Queen

The first volume of **Wellness Activities for Youth** helps leaders teach children and teenagers about wellness with a whole person approach, a "no put-down" rule, and most of all, an emphasis on FUN. The concepts include:

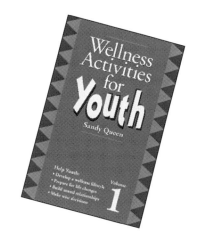

- values
- stress and coping
- self-esteem
- personal well-being
- social wellness

WELLNESS ACTIVITIES FOR YOUTH
WORKSHEET MASTERS

Complete packages of full-size (8 1/2" x 11") photocopy masters that include all the worksheets and handouts from **Wellness Activities for Youth Volumes 1 and 2** are available to you. Use the masters for easy duplication of the handouts for each participant.

❑ **WY1 / Wellness Activities for Youth Volume 1 / $19.95**
❑ **WY2 / Wellness Activities for Youth Volume 2 / $19.95**
❑ **WY1W / Wellness Activities for Youth V. 1 Worksheet Masters / $9.95**
❑ **WY2W / Wellness Activities for Youth V. 2 Worksheet Masters / $9.95**

©1994 Whole Person Press 210 W Michigan Duluth MN 55802   (800) 247-6789

WORKING WITH WOMEN'S GROUPS
Volumes 1 & 2

Louise Yolton Eberhardt

The two volumes of **Working with Women's Groups** have been completely revised and updated. These exercises will help women explore issues that are of perennial concern as well as today's hot topics.

Volume 1:
- consciousness-raising
- self-discovery
- assertiveness training

Volume 2:
- sexuality issues
- women of color
- leadership skills training

WORKING WITH WOMEN'S GROUPS WORKSHEET MASTERS

Complete packages of full-size (8 1/2" x 11") photocopy masters that include all the worksheets and handouts from **Working with Women's Groups volume 1 and 2** are available to you. Use the masters for easy duplication of the handouts for each participant.

- ❑ **WG1 / Working with Women's Groups—Volume 1 / $24.95**
- ❑ **WG2 / Working with Women's Groups—Volume 2 / $24.95**
- ❑ **WG1W / Working with Women's Groups—Volume 1 Worksheet Masters / $9.95**
- ❑ **WG2W / Working with Women's Groups—Volume 2 Worksheet Masters / $9.95**

WORKING WITH MEN'S GROUPS

Roger Karsk and Bill Thomas

Also revised and updated, this volume is a valuable resource for anyone working with men's groups. The exercises cover a variety of topics, including:

- self discovery
- parenting
- conflict
- intimacy

- ❑ **MG / Working with Men's Groups / $24.95**
- ❑ **MGW / Working with Men's Groups Worksheet Masters / $9.95**

WORKING WITH GROUPS FROM DYSFUNCTIONAL FAMILIES

Cheryl Hetherington

This collection of 29 proven group activities is designed to heal the pain that results from growing up in or living in a dysfunctional family. With these exercises you can:

- promote healing
- build self-esteem
- encourage sharing
- help participants acknowledge their
   feelings

WORKING WITH GROUPS FROM DYSFUNCTIONAL FAMILIES REPRODUCIBLE WORKSHEET MASTERS

A complete package of full-size (8 1/2" x 11") photocopy masters that include all the worksheets and handouts from **Working with Groups from Dysfunctional Families** is available to you. Use the masters for easy duplication of the handouts for each participant.

- ❑ **DFH / Working with Groups from Dysfunctional Families / $24.95**
- ❑ **DFW / Dysfunctional Families Worksheet Masters / $9.95**

PLAYFUL ACTIVITIES FOR POWERFUL PRESENTATIONS

Bruce Williamson

This book contains 40 fun exercises designed to fit any group or topic. These exercises will help you:

- build teamwork
- encourage laughter and playfulness
- relieve stress and tension
- free up the imaginations of participants

- ❑ **PAP / Playful Activities for Powerful Presentations
   $19.95**

©1994 Whole Person Press 210 W Michigan Duluth MN 55802   (800) 247-6789

STRUCTURED EXERCISES
IN STRESS MANAGEMENT—VOLUMES 1-4
Nancy Loving Tubesing, EdD and Donald A. Tubesing, PhD, Editors

Each book in this four-volume series contains 36 ready-to-use teaching modules that involve the participant—as a whole person—in learning how to manage stress more effectively.

Each exercise is carefully designed by top stress-management professionals. Instructions are clearly written and field-tested so that even beginning trainers can smoothly lead a group through warm-up and closure, reflection and planning, and action and interaction—all with minimum preparation time.

Each Stress Handbook is brimming with practical ideas that you can weave into your own teaching designs or mix and match to develop new programs for varied settings, audiences, and time frames. In each volume you'll find **Icebreakers, Stress Assessments, Management Strategies, Skill Builders, Action Planners, Closing Processes** and **Group Energizers**—all with a special focus on stress management.

STRUCTURED EXERCISES
IN WELLNESS PROMOTION—VOLUMES 1-4
Nancy Loving Tubesing, EdD and Donald A. Tubesing, PhD, Editors

Discover the Wellness Handbooks—from the wellness pioneers at Whole Person Associates. Each volume in this innovative series includes 36 experiential learning activities that focus on whole person health—body, mind, spirit, emotions, relationships, and lifestyle.

The exercises, developed by an interdisciplinary pool of leaders in the wellness movement nationwide, actively encourage people to adopt wellness-oriented attitudes and to develop more responsible self-care patterns.

All process designs in the Wellness Handbooks are clearly explained and have been thoroughly field-tested with diverse audiences so that trainers can use them with confidence. **Icebreakers, Wellness Explorations, Self-Care Strategies, Action Planners, Closings** and **Group Energizers** are all ready-to-go—including reproducible worksheets, scripts, and chalktalk outlines—for the busy professional who wants to develop unique wellness programs without spending oodles of time in preparation.

STRUCTURED EXERCISES IN STRESS AND WELLNESS ARE AVAILABLE IN TWO FORMATS

LOOSE-LEAF FORMAT (8 1/2" x 11")

The loose-leaf, 3-ring binder format provides you with maximum flexiblity. The binder gives you plenty of room to add your own adaptations, workshop outlines, or notes right where you need them. The index tabs offer quick and easy access to each section of exercises, and the generous margins allow plenty of room for notes. In addition an extra set of the full-size worksheets and handouts are packaged separately for convenient duplication.

SOFTCOVER FORMAT (6" x 9")

The softcover format is a perfect companion to the loose-leaf version. This smaller book fits easily into your briefcase or bag, and the binding has been designed to remain open on your desk or lectern. Worksheets and handouts can be enlarged and photocopied for distribution to your participants, or you can purchase sets of worksheet masters.

WORKSHEET MASTERS

The Worksheet Masters for the two Structured Exercise series offer full-size (8 1/2" x 11") photocopy masters. All of the worksheets and handouts for each volume are reproduced in easy-to-read print with professional graphics. All you need to do to complete your workshop preparation is run them through a copier.

Structured Exercises in Stress Management

- ❑ **Loose-Leaf Edition—Volume 1-4 / $54.95 each**
- ❑ **Softcover Edition—Volume 1-4 / $29.95 each**
- ❑ **Worksheet Masters—Volume 1-4 / $9.95 each**

Structured Exercises in Wellness Promotion

- ❑ **Loose-Leaf Edition—Volume 1-4 / $54.95 each**
- ❑ **Softcover Edition—Volume 1-4 / $29.95 each**
- ❑ **Worksheet Masters—Volume 1-4 / $9.95 each**

©1994 Whole Person Press 210 W Michigan Duluth MN 55802   (800) 247-6789

WORKSHOPS-IN-A-BOOK

KICKING YOUR STRESS HABITS:
A Do-it-yourself Guide to Coping with Stress
Donald A. Tubesing, PhD

Over a quarter of a million people have found ways to deal with their everyday stress by using **Kicking Your Stress Habits**. This workshop-in-a-book actively involves the reader in assessing stressful patterns and developing more effective coping strategies with helpful "Stop and Reflect" sections in each chapter.

The 10-step planning process and 20 skills for managing stress make **Kicking Your Stress Habits** an ideal text for stress management classes in many different settings, from hospitals to universities and for a wide variety of groups.

❏ **K / Kicking Your Stress Habits / 14.95**

SEEKING YOUR HEALTHY BALANCE:
A Do-it-yourself Guide to Whole Person Well-being
Donald A. Tubesing, PhD and Nancy Loving Tubesing, EdD

Where can you find the time and energy to "do it all" without sacrificing your health and well-being? **Seeking Your Healthy Balance** helps the reader discover how to make changes toward a more balanced lifestyle by learning effective ways to juggle work, self, and others; clarifying self-care options; and discovering and setting their own personal priorities.

Seeking Your Healthy Balance asks the questions and helps readers find their own answers.

❏ **HB / Seeking Your Healthy Balance / 14.95**

©1994 Whole Person Press 210 W Michigan Duluth MN 55802   (800) 247-6789

RELAXATION RESOURCES

Many trainers and workshop leaders have discovered the benefits of relaxation and visualization in healing the body, mind, and spirit.

30 SCRIPTS FOR RELAXATION, IMAGERY, AND INNER HEALING
Julie Lusk

These two volumes are collections of relaxation scripts created by trainers for trainers. The 30 scripts in each of the two volumes have been professionally-tested and fine-tuned so they are ready to use for both novice and expert trainers.

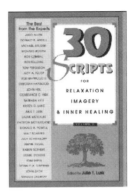

Help your participants change their behavior, enhance their self-esteem, discover inner, private places, and heal themselves through simple trainer-led guided imagery scripts. Both volumes include information on how to use the scripts, suggestions for tailoring them to your specific needs and audience, and information on how to successfully incorporate guided imagery into your existing programs.

❑ 30S / 30 Scripts for Relaxation, Imagery, and Inner Healing—Volume 1 / $19.95
❑ 30S2 / 30 Scripts for Relaxation, Imagery, and Inner Healing—Volume 2 / $19.95

INQUIRE WITHIN
Andrew Schwartz

Use visualization to make positive changes in your life. The 24 visualization experiences in **Inquire Within** will help participants enhance their creativity, heal inner pain, learn to relax, and deal with conflict. Each visualization includes questions at the end of the process that encourage deeper reflection and a better understanding of the exercise and the response it invokes.

❑ IW / Inquire Within / $19.95

©1994 Whole Person Press 210 W Michigan Duluth MN 55802   (800) 247-6789

RELAXATION AUDIOTAPES

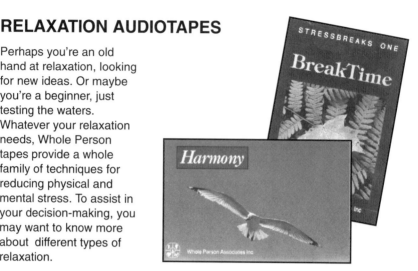

Perhaps you're an old hand at relaxation, looking for new ideas. Or maybe you're a beginner, just testing the waters. Whatever your relaxation needs, Whole Person tapes provide a whole family of techniques for reducing physical and mental stress. To assist in your decision-making, you may want to know more about different types of relaxation.

We offer six different types of relaxation techniques in our twenty-one tapes. The Whole Person series ranges from simple breathing and stretching exercises, to classic autogenic and progressive relaxation sequences, to guided meditations and whimsical daydreams. All are carefully crafted to promote whole person relaxation—body, mind, and spirit. We also provide a line of music-only tapes, composed specifically for relaxation.

SENSATIONAL RELAXATION

When stress piles up, it becomes a heavy load both physically and emotionally. These full-length relaxation experiences will teach you techniques that can be used whenever you feel that stress is getting out of control. Choose one you like and repeat it daily until it becomes second nature then recall that technique whenever you need it.

- ❏ **CD / Countdown to Relaxation / $9.95**
- ❏ **DS / Daybreak / Sundown / $9.95**
- ❏ **TDB / Take a Deep Breath / $9.95**
- ❏ **RLX / Relax . . . Let Go . . . Relax / $9.95**
- ❏ **SRL / StressRelease / $9.95**
- ❏ **WRM / Warm and Heavy / $9.95**

STRESS BREAKS

Do you need a short energy booster or a quick stress reliever? If you don't know what type of relaxation you like, or if you are new to guided relaxation techniques, try one of our Stress Breaks for a quick refocusing or change of pace any time of the day.

- ❏ **BT / BreakTime / $9.95**
- ❏ **NT / Natural Tranquilizers / $9.95**

DAYDREAMS

Escape from the stress around you with guided tours to beautiful places. Picture yourself traveling to the ocean, sitting in a park, luxuriating in the view from the majestic mountains, or enjoying the solitude and serenity of a cozy cabin. The 10-minute escapes included in our Daydream tapes will lead your imagination away from your everyday cares so you can resume your tasks relaxed and comforted.

> ❏ **DD1 / Daydreams 1: Getaways / $9.95**
> ❏ **DD2 / Daydreams 2: Peaceful Places / $9.95**

GUIDED MEDITATION

Take a step beyond relaxation and discover the connection between body and mind with guided meditation. The imagery in our full-length meditations will help you discover your strengths, find healing, make positive life changes, and recognize your inner wisdom.

> ❏ **IH / Inner Healing / $9.95**
> ❏ **PE / Personal Empowering / $9.95**
> ❏ **HBT / Healthy Balancing / $9.95**
> ❏ **SPC / Spiritual Centering / $9.95**

WILDERNESS DAYDREAMS

Discover the healing power of nature with the four tapes in the Wilderness Daydreams series. The eight special journeys will transport you from your harried, stressful surroundings to the peaceful serenity of words and water.

> ❏ **WD1 / Canoe / Rain / $9.95**
> ❏ **WD2 / Island /Spring / $9.95**
> ❏ **WD3 / Campfire / Stream / $9.95**
> ❏ **WD4 / Sailboat / Pond / $9.95**

MUSIC ONLY

No relaxation program would be complete without relaxing melodies that can be played as background to a prepared script or that can be enjoyed as you practice a technique you have already learned. Steven Eckels composed his melodies specifically for relaxation. These "musical prayers for healing" will calm your body, mind, and spirit.

> ❏ **T / Tranquility / $9.95**
> ❏ **H / Harmony / $9.95**
> ❏ **S / Serenity / $9.95**

Titles can be combined for discounts!

QUANTITY DISCOUNT			
1 - 9	10 - 49	50 - 99	100+
$9.95	$8.95	$7.96	CALL

©1994 Whole Person Press 210 W Michigan Duluth MN 55802   (800) 247-6789

ORDER FORM

Name _____

Address _____

City _____

State/Zip _____

Area Code/Telephone _____

Please make checks payable to:
Whole Person Associates Inc
210 West Michigan
Duluth MN 55802-1908
FAX: 1-218-727-0505
TOLL FREE: 1-800-247-6789

Books / Workshops-In-A-Book

___ Kicking Your Stress Habits	$14.95	_____
___ Seeking Your Healthy Balance	$14.95	_____

Structured Exercises in Stress Management Series—Volumes 1-4

___ Stress Softcover Edition .... Vol 1 ___ Vol 2 ___ Vol 3 ___ Vol 4 ___ $29.95 _____
___ Stress Loose-Leaf Edition .... Vol 1 ___ Vol 2 ___ Vol 3 ___ Vol 4 ___ $54.95 _____
___ Stress Worksheet Masters ...... Vol 1 ___ Vol 2 ___ Vol 3 ___ Vol 4 ___ $9.95 _____

Structured Exercises in Wellness Promotion Series—Volumes 1-4

___ Wellness Softcover Edition .... Vol 1 ___ Vol 2 ___ Vol 3 ___ Vol 4 ___ $29.95 _____
___ Wellness Loose-Leaf Edition ..... Vol 1 ___ Vol 2 ___ Vol 3 ___ Vol 4 ___ $54.95 _____
___ Wellness Worksheet Masters .... Vol 1 ___ Vol 2 ___ Vol 3 ___ Vol 4 ___ $9.95 _____

Group Process Resources

___ Playful Activities for Powerful Presentations	$19.95	_____
___ Working with Groups from Dysfunctional Families	$24.95	_____
___ Working with Groups from Dysfunctional Families Worksheet Masters	$9.95	_____
___ Working with Women's Groups .... Vol 1 ___ Vol 2 ___	$24.95	_____
___ Working with Women's Groups Worksheet Masters ...... Vol 1 ___ Vol 2 ___	$9.95	_____
___ Working with Men's Groups	$24.95	_____
___ Working with Men's Groups Worksheet Masters	$9.95	_____
___ Wellness Activities for Youth .... Vol 1 ___ Vol 2 ___	$19.95	_____
___ Wellness Activities for Youth Worksheet Masters ...... Vol 1 ___ Vol 2 ___	$9.95	_____

Relaxation Audiotapes

___ BreakTime	$ 9.95	_____
___ Countdown to Relaxation	$ 9.95	_____
___ Daybreak/Sundown	$ 9.95	_____
___ Daydreams 1: Getaways	$ 9.95	_____
___ Daydreams 2: Peaceful Places	$ 9.95	_____
___ Harmony (music only)	$ 9.95	_____
___ Healthy Balancing	$ 9.95	_____
___ Inner Healing	$ 9.95	_____
___ Natural Tranquilizers	$ 9.95	_____
___ Personal Empowering	$ 9.95	_____
___ Relax . . . Let Go . . . Relax	$ 9.95	_____
___ Serenity (music only)	$ 9.95	_____
___ Spiritual Centering	$ 9.95	_____
___ StressRelease	$ 9.95	_____
___ Take a Deep Breath	$ 9.95	_____
___ Tranquility (music only)	$ 9.95	_____
___ Warm and Heavy	$ 9.95	_____
___ Wilderness DD 1: Canoe/Rain	$ 9.95	_____
___ Wilderness DD 2: Island/Spring	$ 9.95	_____
___ Wilderness DD 3: Campfire/Stream	$ 9.95	_____
___ Wilderness DD 4: Sailboat/Pond	$ 9.95	_____

Relaxation Resources

___ 30 Scripts—Volume 1	$19.95	_____
___ 30 Scripts—Volume 2	$19.95	_____
___ Inquire Within	$19.95	_____

My check is enclosed. **(US funds only)**

Please charge my_____Visa _____Mastercard

_____

Exp date _____

Signature _____

SUBTOTAL	_____
TAX (MN residents 6.5%)	_____
7% GST-Canadian customers only	_____
**SHIPPING	_____
GRAND TOTAL	_____

800-247-6789

** **SHIPPING.** $5.00 ($8.00 outside U.S.)
Please call us for quotes on UPS 3rd Day,
2nd Day or Next Day Air.

About Whole Person Associates

At Whole Person Associates, we're 100% committed to providing stress and wellness materials that involve participants and have a "whole person" focus—body, mind, spirit, and relationships.

That's our mission and it's very important to us—but it doesn't tell the whole story. Behind the products in our catalog is a company full of people—and *that's* what really makes us who we are.

ABOUT THE OWNERS

Whole Person Associates was created by the vision of two people: Donald A. Tubesing, PhD, and Nancy Loving Tubesing, EdD. Since way back in 1970, Don and Nancy have been active in the stress management/wellness promotion movement—consulting, leading seminars, writing, and publishing. Most of our early products were the result of their creativity and expertise.

Living proof that you can "stay evergreen," Don and Nancy remain the driving force behind the company and are still very active in developing new products that touch people's lives.

ABOUT THE COMPANY

Whole Person Associates was "born" in Duluth, Minnesota, and we remain committed to our lovely city on the shore of Lake Superior. All of our operations are here, which makes communication between departments much easier! We've grown since our beginnings, but at a steady pace—we're interested in sustainable growth that allows us to keep our down-to-earth orientation.

We put the same high quality into every product we offer, translating the best of current research into practical, accessible, easy-to-use materials. In this way we can create the best possible resources to help our customers teach about stress management and wellness promotion.

We also strive to treat our customers as we would like to be treated. If we fall short of our goals in any way, please let us know.

ABOUT OUR EMPLOYEES

Speaking of down-to-earth, that's a requirement for each and every one of our employees. We're all product consultants, which means that anyone who answers the phone can probably answer your questions (if they can't, they'll find someone who can.)

We focus on helping you find the products that fit your needs. And we've found that the best way to do that is to hire friendly and resourceful people.

©1994 Whole Person Press 210 W Michigan Duluth MN 55802   (800) 247-6789

ABOUT OUR ASSOCIATES

Who are the "associates" in Whole Person Associates? They're the trainers, authors, musicians, and others who have developed much of the material you see on these pages. We're always on the lookout for high-quality products that reflect our "whole person" philosophy and fill a need for our customers.

Most of our products were developed by experts who are the tops in their fields, and we're very proud to be associated with them.

ABOUT OUR CUSTOMERS

Finally, we wouldn't have a reason to exist without you, our customers. We've met some of you, and we've talked to many more of you on the phone. We are always aware that without you, there would be no Whole Person Associates.

That's why we'd love to hear from you! Let us know what you think of our products—how you use them in your work, what additional products you'd like to see, and what shortcomings you've noted. Write us or call on our toll-free line. We look forward to hearing from you!

TRAINER'S NOTES

TRAINER'S NOTES